Sexing the Animal in a Posthumanist World

This pioneering collection of essays unpacks the complex discursive and embodied relationships between humans and animals, contributing to a more informed understanding of both human–animal relations and the role of language in social processes. Focusing on the example of shark–human interactions, the book draws on forms of analysis from multimodality and critical discourse studies to examine the representations of this relationship across visual arts, popular media, and the natural sciences, each viewed through a critical feminist lens. The combined effect highlights the significance of the emergent turn to posthumanism in applied linguistics and its role in fostering more engaged discussions around broader contemporary social issues, including environmental degradation and climate change on the one hand, and resurgent feminism and challenges to normative heterosexuality on the other. Paving the way for new forms of writing and language for a post-anthropocentric age, this volume is essential reading for students and scholars in applied linguistics, gender studies, sociolinguistics, human–animal studies, and environmental humanities.

Roslyn Appleby is a senior lecturer in Applied Linguistics and TESOL at the University of Technology Sydney. Her research focuses on the cultural politics of gender and sexuality and she is the author of *Men and Masculinities in Global English Language Teaching* (Palgrave Macmillan), and *ELT, Gender, and International Development* (Multilingual Matters).

Sexing the Animal in a Posthumanist World

A Critical Feminist Approach

Roslyn Appleby

Routledge
Taylor & Francis Group

LONDON AND NEW YORK

First published 2019 by Routledge

2 Park Square, Milton Park, Abingdon, Oxon, OX14 4RN

605 Third Avenue, New York, NY 10017

Routledge is an imprint of the Taylor & Francis Group, an informa business

First issued in paperback 2020

Library of Congress Cataloging-in-Publication Data
Names: Appleby, Roslyn, author.
Title: Sexing the animal in a posthumanist world : a critical feminist
    approach / by Roslyn Appleby.
Description: London ; New York : Routledge, 2019. | Includes
    bibliographical references and index.
Identifiers: LCCN 2019010286 | ISBN 9781138575752 (hardback)
Subjects: LCSH: Ecofeminism. | Ecolinguistics. | Human-animal
    relationships. | Feminist theory.
Classification: LCC HQ1233 .A79 2019 | DDC 304.2082—dc23
LC record available at https://lccn.loc.gov/2019010286

ISBN: 978-1-138-57575-2 (hbk)
ISBN: 978-0-367-72882-3 (pbk)

Typeset in Times New Roman
by Apex CoVantage, LLC

Contents

Figures

Acknowledgements

My journey to understand and become entangled with the life of sharks began with a January project in 2013, when I started swimming with a group of folks who, each day, enjoy an early morning swim in the Pacific Ocean. My thanks go to many friends in this group who have inspired and shared my love of life in the ocean. For sharing photos and conversations about our ocean experience, special thanks go to swim buddies Mauricio Fuentes, Elaine de Jager, Nick Dawkins, Sharnie Connell, and Fiona Dobrijevich.

Among my colleagues, I owe thanks to those who have shared my enthusiasm for life beyond academia, in the more-than-human world. In particular, my thanks go to Keiko Yasukawa, for endless conversations about dogs, camels, goats, and all other creatures; Alastair Pennycook for enthusiastic conversations about fish, sharks, and nudibranchs; and Margaret Somerville for conversations about the delights of playing with water and entanglements in the vibrant materiality of life. Thanks also to colleagues, including Guy Cook, Mary Bucholtz, Phillip Armstrong, and Phiona Stanley, who have listened to me talk about sharks, sex, and gender at various conferences, and have offered encouragement to pursue my ideas.

And finally, my gratitude and thanks to three very special people, Tom, Nick, and Lucy, for the laughter and love which are necessary ingredients for any life project.

1 Introduction

06:15, Manly Beach, Australia, Spring. I wade into the surf, alone, through a tangle of kelp. Three friends are just returning from their swim and greet me: There's a huge shark out there, they say. Where? I ask, what sort of shark? It's around the point, a grey nurse, beautiful. I hesitate. Okay, so now's the decision: Do I wade back to shore, or do I plunge forward, into the ocean I love, and towards the shark? I take a deep breath, dive through the waves, swim out to the point, then turn south towards Shelly. Then over the rock platform that stretches out from the point, covered in a mass of weeds and cunjivoi. I swim near the edge of the platform where it drops deep into a sandy bottom. And there below me is the grey nurse. Big, calm, gliding along surrounded by a following of tiny fishes, shimmering around the shark's body like a sequinned gown. Magnificent. I made the right decision.

In all my childhood years of swimming at Australian beaches, the grey nurse shark, *Carcharius taurus*, had a reputation as a man-eater due to its fierce appearance and large size. It wasn't until the 1990s that the grey nurse was recognised as a shark that posed no threat to swimmers, surfers or divers, unless provoked. But through those years of human ignorance, the shark's undeserved reputation became a justification for indiscriminate killing, to the point where the grey nurse shark is now officially classified as a critically endangered or threatened species. Their numbers are so low that individual animals are now failing to find mates and successfully reproduce. Further south from here, and in other places around the world, the grey nurse is considered to be extinct. Human activities targeting sharks, such as finning, commercial and recreational fishing, and the installation of beach nets and drum lines, pose a far greater threat to these gentle creatures than they have ever posed to us.

For me, as an ocean swimmer, the sharks are a gift. Each one is, to use a phrase popularised by Tom Regan (1983), the individual subject of a life, with a unique life story full of experiences and challenges. Yet their fate is emblematic of the biological annihilation of wildlife—the sixth great extinction—brought about by human activities. Through their own lively, embodied, elusive magnificence, they open a doorway into the wider natural world where humans can again, with respectful care, become aware and entangled in beauty. Sharks can speak to us about themselves, and they can also offer insights into the ways in which humans think and act in the world. Swimming with sharks is at the centre of this book.

In this opening chapter, I discuss some of the broader theoretical context for my shark musings. If these underlying ideas and movements are not of interest, feel free to swim onwards to Chapter 2.

The essays in this book grapple with two issues that have gained a particular urgency and agency in recent years. First, as inhabitants of a unique planet we face pressing issues of environmental degradation, unprecedented species extinctions, and a warming biosphere that threatens planetary survival. These are massive problems that together form an unprecedented, human-generated, planetary environmental crisis. At the same time, on the intimate scale of fleshy human bodies, a new wave of feminist activity has been provoked by ongoing problems to do with gender and sexuality: rage

Figure 1.1 Grey Nurse Shark
Source: (photo Fioina Dobrijevich)

against sexual harassment, oppression, coercion, control, and misrepresentation that have troubled girls and women for generations yet have re-emerged as points of contention in a new age.

Finding ways to address these transdisciplinary problems from within applied linguistics is an ongoing project. One sphere of problems, captured in phrases such as climate change in the Anthropocene, seems too vast, too impersonal for individuals to contend with or amend. A second sphere of problems is intimate, sticky, embodied, and personal, but equally deeply disturbing. How can we bring these two perspectives together? How can we explore one, without losing sight of the other? Both questions bring me to thinking in a domain where language and matter come together, where representation and flesh intersect yet never fully consume, exhaust, or explain each other. To borrow from Barad (2007) I'm aiming for a lively practice of meeting the world halfway.

Language and the Material of Life

Having lived my entire life with a body that has been classified as female, I have never been entirely convinced that human language could hold the sole key to understanding my lived experience. When I returned to university as a doctoral student in my middle years, I was faced with a frame of contemporary thinking that privileged language and discourse as the only feasible ways of understanding lived experience. And yet I always felt that the visceral experience of the lived body, through ageing and hunger, for example, or through female genital mutilation, or through childbirth, was an experience *of the body*, regardless of the language we chose to describe, interpret, theorise, or represent those experiences. Looking back, my untutored response was no doubt theoretically naïve, but my gut reaction was also borne of a body that had never been completely fooled by a certain academic elite that attempts to dictate what and how my body makes meaning. Now, with the weight of contemporary theoretical interest in new materialism and a resurgence in feminist politics, I return to those original intuitions that emphasise the significance of the body, of embodied knowledge, woven together with a richer understanding of language and how language impacts experience.

Deconstruction of the material–discourse binary, and the dethroning of the privileged status accorded to language, are central to the broad range of approaches that fall under the label 'new materialism'. As MacLure (2013, p. 659) observes, new materialisms contest the notion of nature and the natural body as an inert background against which 'humanist adventures of culture are played out' and argue that language—and the status granted to linguistic representation of the material world—has 'rendered material realties inaccessible behind the linguistic or discourse systems that purportedly construct or "represent" them'. This is not to ignore the significant effects that language and discourses have in our understanding and experience of the world. But rather, it is to recognise that language has been 'granted too much power' such that 'every "thing"—even materiality—is turned into a matter of language or some other form of cultural representation' (Barad, 2007, p. 132).

New materialisms, while theoretically diverse, are united in their insistence on the significance of matter and materiality in social and cultural practices, and they place human language as an actor of 'second-order intervention' in the entangled, dynamic, proliferating, emergent liveliness of life (MacLure, 2013, p. 659). Capturing something of this dynamic liveliness has been the focus of researchers working with non-representational ethnographies that emphasise 'the fleeting, viscous, lively, embodied, material, more-than-human, precognitive, non-discursive dimensions of spatially and temporally complex lifeworlds' (Vannini, 2014, p. 317).

The resultant lively mixtures of language and matter, of animate and inanimate objects that might form the focus of our studies have been called by different names, including assemblages, entanglements, and actor networks. In these new materialist assemblages, human and non-human actants are presented on a less hierarchical plane, with technological and natural materialities accepted as participating actors, alongside and within human actors, as 'vitalities, trajectories and powers irreducible to the meanings, intentions, or symbolic values humans invest in them' (Bennett, 2010, p. 47). A decentring of humans in the ordering of the world is evident in the thinking around new materialisms. This way of thinking about our place in the world defies both human exceptionalism and the place granted to language as the key feature that separates humans from other creatures, while at the same time demanding accountability for the effect of humans and human language on and in the world (Barad, 2007; Pennycook, 2018).

Two particular streams within new materialism are of interest to me in this collection of essays. The first is my interest in human relationships with other non-human animals; the second is my interest in the deleterious effects of humans on the broader natural world. Both fields of interest are then inflected by my curiosity and concern with feminist understandings of the ways in which human readings of sex and gender play out in our relationships with the more-than-human-world. In the following sections I begin to outline some of these interests and concerns.

Starting With a Dog

Much of my thinking about human relationships with other animals surfaced in vivid form when I inherited a dog, a bitch called Sista. There is much that one learns through a close relationship with an individual dog.

I recognise that so-called animal 'pets' have attracted a deal of disparaging and dismissive comment in academic discourse, particularly directed at women who have explored in intimate and loving detail their relationships with female dogs (Haraway, 2003 is perhaps the best known of this genre). Indeed, women writing about their lives with female canines have experienced a peculiar type of backlash, despite the ground that such writing breaks in terms of extending feminist forms of embodied political critique and thereby contributing to significant developments in theories of sex, gender, and species:

> they move narrative beyond the abstract model of the lone 'authoritative' human individual, reframing feminist politics as intra-active, even trans-species, from the ground up.
>
> (McHugh, 2012, p. 616)

I also acknowledge some of the grave concerns and ambiguous ethics that surround human relationships with animals kept as pets or, in more recent parlance, as animal companions (Pierce, 2016). Yet to only highlight the negative aspects of pet 'ownership', to use the legal term, is to underestimate what this close relationship can offer to both sides of a human–canine entanglement. Given the erasure of most non-human animals in contemporary Western life (Stibbe, 2012) it is through human relationships with such animals in our domestic lives that we might first have the opportunity to gain some insight into the intelligence, rich emotions, and significance of those fellow creaturely beings with whom we share the world.

In my own relationship with Sista, flesh and language came together in a world of inter-species learning. When, as a teenager, she first came to live with me, she sat for days with her back to the wall, looking rather stoic and sullen, observing me as I went about daily life. Before long it seemed to me that we were developing a shared visual and aural grammar. Perhaps she recognised the meaning of the various clothes I wore at particular times of day: jeans and sneakers meant I was going out for a walk, a signalling hand in her direction meant she could follow me; pyjamas meant bedtime. Sista's language for me was equally clear: her incessant knocking on the door was her summons for me to open it, her frantic tantrums downstairs at night were a demand to join me upstairs to sleep under my bed (Appleby, 2012). Sista insisted that I take her sentience seriously, that I respond to her as a creature divided from me only by a flimsy veil of speciesism. From that time onwards, it was impossible to ignore my intimate interrelationship with other creatures in a more-than-human world.

I wrote about my experience of human–dog communication from my personal perspective, and also from my position as a scholar with an interest in sociocultural linguistics (Appleby, 2012). From a different disciplinary perspective, Pierce (2016), a bioethicist, expands on this notion of inter-species language, observing that 'the ability of humans and dogs to communicate with each other is nothing short of remarkable' (p. 41). Being able to communicate well, says Pierce, 'is the foundation for a successful relationship' but 'learning to communicate with an animal companion is a *bit like learning a foreign language*' (p. 40, emphasis added) giving rise to misunderstandings that are similar to those that can occur between speakers of different human languages. However, Pierce also notes that words, as a component of language, are relatively insignificant in communication: humans are a highly visual species who rely on facial expression, bodily movements, and gaze in order to apprehend what we really need to know. Equally, the ability of a dog to follow a human gaze, to respond to a pointing hand, or to direct human attention and action through their own non-verbal practices are some of the most obvious semiotic signs that characterise human–dog communicative repertoires.

It seems rather churlish, then, to resist or to sneer at descriptions of human–dog non-verbal communication and understanding, to dismiss such accounts as naively anthropomorphic or sentimentalising; nor is it reasonable to privilege human speech at the expense of serious engagement with equally articulate non-linguistic forms of inter-species communication. Bob Plant (2011) poses a series of questions that bring a sharper focus to the issue of hierarchies in species' communicative repertoires. If we take non-linguistic communication and behaviour seriously, then why, asks Plant, should we elevate the human's '*hello*', expressed through a smiling face, an open body, so far above the pre-linguistic, though manifestly expressed '*welcome*' expressed in posture and movement by a dog in response to her human companion? And why would a human cry of pain only be ethically significant if it could be replaced by verbal equivalent such as 'That hurts!' or 'I'm in pain!'. By extension, then, 'we must ask what, ethically speaking, distinguishes the *human's* cry of pain from the *animal's*?', and so he concludes that the human's and the animal's forms of communication are only '*different in kind*' (Plant, 2011, p. 61).

My relationship with Sista opened a door into a new world of events, phenomena, and entanglements that exceed the representational capacity of language. Something in the animals we encounter resists analysis through the conventions of coding, categorising, and testing, refuses to render up meaning in linguistic form, though given our limited conventions of human communication we might still attempt to do just that. Our inability to speak their language invites us to *listen*, to *watch*, and engage in other ways: the ultimately undecidable, indeterminate nature of their communication brings apprehension and interpretation to a halt in a whirlwind of unanswered questions, frustrating our attempts at representation and exposing the limits of reductive explanations and rationality (MacLure, 2013). We need to explore our relationship with other species in ways that search for meaning in more than words, through the body, experiential encounters, emotions, arts, and senses.

Humans, Other Animals, and Gender

The field of human–animal studies, and the broader field of environmentalism, have been informed by a strong tradition within feminism that is concerned with challenging humanist and patriarchal assumptions about gender, animals, and animality. Such prejudices include the notion that both women and animals are 'avatars of nature', debased by a shared association with body over mind, emotions over reason, and object rather than subject status (Fraiman, 2012, p. 99). In contrast, a prevailing discourse of normative masculinity rests on the construction of men as rational subjects, who therefore naturally dominate and consume women and animals alike.

Rising to prominence in the 1980s, ecofeminist concerns have also encompassed the intersecting connections among sexism, racism, classism, colonialism, speciesism, and the environment, together with a critique of the normative, masculinist model of mastery (Plumwood, 1993) that has shaped Western culture's relationship with nature. Yet from the late 1990s a backlash against 'animal ecofeminism' charged the ecofeminist movement with bias towards ethnocentric gender essentialism, and the focus of mainstream feminist scholarship turned towards more situated, human-centric concerns in the new millennium (Gaard, 2011, pp. 35–36). Based primarily on objections to the woman–nature connection and goddess spirituality strands of ecofeminism, this backlash had, according to Gaard (2011), mistaken the part for the whole, thereby discrediting and marginalising a diverse, complex, and theoretically grounded environmentalist scholarship.

More recently, however, the critique of humanism and masculinist mastery offered by ecofeminism has been revitalised with the emergence of feminist new materialism, which advances a life-affirming sense of the agencies expressed in a material world and a renewed theoretical engagement with embodiment and material relations (Garlick, 2017). As discussed previously, new materialism shifts the critical focus of feminism outwards towards the more-than-human world, beyond poststructuralism and social constructionism, by reconceptualising the dynamic and creative *intra-actions* (Barad, 2007) amongst material, discursive, animal, and technological beings, objects, and phenomena.

In a related confluence of interests, the link between feminist concerns, environmentalism, and animal studies has been revitalised in the turn to posthumanism and its particular focus on addressing the destructive effects of the Anthropocene. In this regard, and echoing earlier ecofeminist politics, Rosi Braidotti (2013) has reiterated an alignment between female embodiment and the wider scope of planetary life forms, also known as *zoe*. For Braidotti, a zoe-centred egalitarianism is at the core of a productive, affirmative post-anthropocentric movement that aims to address contemporary ecological crises.

However, the project of unleashing the affirmative forces of post-anthropocentrism and displacing species hierarchies faces significant challenges. One key challenge lies in the discursive grip of language on our ways of thinking and doing in relation to other species and the world. To advance a zoe-centric project, applied linguists have a role in interrogating the deleterious ways in which language and other semiotic resources define and shape relationships between human and non-human species (see, for example, Cook, 2015), and exploring alternative ways of using language to generate more productive engagements and entanglements with the more-than-human world (Appleby & Pennycook, 2017). An important body of work in ecolinguistics has focussed on this challenge.

The particular type of ecolinguistics that interests me in this project is that which critically analyses discourse in order to illuminate the ways in which language shapes our human understanding of, and behaviour within, the more-than-human world. Here, ecology is not used as a metaphor to describe relationships between different human languages, but instead refers to the natural world around us, and to the interdependent web of relationships between humans and non-human animals, and other natural or environmental phenomena on a living planet. Of key importance is Stibbe's (2012, 2014, 2015) extensive work on the role of language in the oppression, exploitation, and erasure of non-human animals and, more broadly, in the degradation and destruction of the ecological systems that support life. Adopting an approach aligned with critical discourse analysis,

> ecolinguistics consists of questioning the stories that underpin our current unsustainable civilization, exposing those stories that are clearly not working, that are leading to ecological destruction and social injustice, and finding new stories that work better in the conditions of the world that we face.
>
> (Stibbe, 2014, p. 117)

For Stibbe, 'stories' refers to discourses, frames, metaphors, and linguistic features that convey particular worldviews. I want to stretch this meaning of stories to explicitly encompass a wide range of multimodal semiotic resources, including still and moving images, objects, people, bodies, places, and artefacts, which together are recognised as comprising contemporary understandings of language, literacy, and texts. In particular, I want to re-engage with narrative, bodies, and images as a means of connecting large, complex, abstract environmental problems with human capacity for sense-making and empathy.

In writing these essays, I'm aware that pushing beyond a focus on human verbal language is a crucial move in tackling the complexity of human–animal relationships. As Calarco (2015, p. 56) points out, the animal world is 'suffice to itself', regardless of whether or not it is brought into language by humans. Perhaps, like Wajcman (2009), we might say that 'from nature, language keeps us at bay', that as human animals 'we are sick with language' and need to indulge a little more in silence. In many respects, then, our task is to push beyond the boundaries of language in order to apprehend, appreciate, or simply accept and respect that which exceeds our limited capacities to pin down and conceptualise the natural world.

Resurgent Feminism

The last thread that knits together the essays in this book is encouraged by the rise of the most recent wave of feminist thought and action. Arguably most recognisable, at least recently in Anglo-American cultures, as the *#metoo movement*, the resurgence of feminism has been evident in political, social, and language-related experiences over recent years.

A groundswell of feminist insurgency had been evident for some years before #metoo. In Australia, the re-emergence of feminist consciousness was marked by the rise and bloody fall of our first (and so far only) female Prime Minister, Julia Gillard between 2010 and 2013, and by a vanguard of women and feminists rising up against the rabble of white male conservative politicians, media shock jocks, and social media trolls determined to destroy women's freedom (Appleby, 2015). Australian attention was again focussed on women's rights when Rosie Batty, a campaigner against domestic violence, was named Australian of the Year in 2015 and brought political and social attention to problems associated with toxic masculinity. Meanwhile, any sense of change or progress in public and private domains has continued to be met with vocal resistance by entrenched conservative powers defending patriarchal privileges.

Feminists were also making a noise across the UK and USA, motivated by a flood of evidence about sexual harassment and patriarchal entitlement across all levels of society. As Deborah Cameron (2017) has pointed out, the word 'feminism' had appeared on *Time* magazine's 2015 list of 'most annoying words that deserved to be banned'. Yet by 2017, 'feminism' was named 'Word of the Year' by the US Merriam-Webster dictionary, based on the number of people searching the word that year. This was a turnaround in fortunes most likely boosted by anti-Trump women's marches and the viral spread of the #metoo campaign.

Rebecca Solnit opened her 2014 essay on 'An insurrectionary year' by proclaiming that she had been 'waiting all my life for what 2014 has brought', because it was 'a year of feminist insurrection against male violence' (published in her 2017 volume, p. 69). And that same year, Solnit closed another essay by linking her feminist sensibilities to the question of our planet's survival:

> I care passionately about the inhabitability of our planet from an environmental perspective, but until it's fully inhabitable by women who can walk freely down the street without the constant fear of trouble and danger, we will labor under practical and psychological burdens that impair our full powers. Which is why, as someone who thinks climate is the most important thing in the world right now, I'm still writing about feminism and women's rights.
>
> (Solnit, 2017, p. 96)

As I write this introduction, in 2018, these twin movements—for planetary survival and women's right to freedom—are burning concerns. The essays in this book address these concerns through a series of questions and discussions about human–shark interactions. In the midst of feminist re-emergence, as the planet's waters warmed and commercial exploitation of sea life accelerated, human interactions with sharks hit a new record high in 2015 when, world-wide, a total of six humans were killed as a result of interactions with sharks. News of this spike in shark-related incidents and fatalities provoked alarm that led to government summits in Australia and inspired a raft of technological interventions aimed at curbing harm to humans. But each year, in Australia alone, at least one woman is killed *every week* by a man she knows, most often a partner or ex-partner, and so many more are assaulted or abused, often by a man they know, sometimes by a total stranger. What sense can we make of these diverse, unrelated happenings? What is it about shark interactions that draw more public attention and fear than everyday violence against women? What can we know about masculinity and feminism by studying our relationship with sharks?

In this collection of essays, I aim to consider such questions through inquiry and exploration in the arts, news media, sport, science, and film fiction.

2   Entangled in the More-Than-Human World

Unloved Others

What does it take, ask Rose and van Dooren (2011, p. 1), 'to capture human imagination in this perilous era, known as the Anthropocene, at a time when much of the diversity of life on Earth is being lost through human action'? They point out that trajectories through life or death depend, for many creatures, on the power to elicit human desire and empathy. Pandas, whales, snow leopards, elephants: some animals may be present in our imagination, eliciting warm feelings of joy or desire, although we may never see them first hand. Others, such as industrially farmed pigs, chicken, or cattle, whose sacrificed bodies we see every day, may be invisible in their fully embodied form, or may elicit sympathy for their suffering as a result of human oppression. Others, such as our pet dogs and cats, we barely see as non-human at all and, at least in many developed countries, lavish love on them as treasured life companions. These desires, loves, and empathies I can understand and share.

But what of the 'unloved others', the 'disliked and actively vilified others' or 'those whose lives become objects of control in the name of conservation, and those whose lives are caught in the cross-hairs of conflicting human desires?' (Rose & van Dooren, 2011, p. 1). What of these non-human animals who are part of our rich Earthly world, but who might be less than beautiful, less than charismatic, or who may, we imagine, pose a threat to our human wellbeing?

Thinking with and about unloved creatures—those that bite, sting, invade or infect, or simply frighten us—requires a combination of embodied, affective, imaginative, and rational faculties and, as such, works across mind–body dualities, blurring the series of binaries that have long separated humans from the rest of the natural world. For some years now, the shark has been the animal who fits, for me, into this complex, awkward category of mixed feeling and emotions. As an ocean swimmer, the shark is also a fellow traveller in my everyday embodied experience of living in the more-than-human world. And, in the words of Dean Crawford (2008), 'Majestic as they may seem when glimpsed in the ocean, sharks are a challenge to love' (p. 8).

Entangled Pedagogies

In spring semester 2015 I was teaching in a university situated in Australia's largest city. One of my course subjects, located in my own discipline of applied linguistics, was a unit designed to develop students' academic language and literacies, inviting students to explore the differences between everyday language and academic English, and to consider the differences between common knowledge and published research in diverse disciplinary fields. The international students taking this elective unit were from non-English speaking backgrounds and were enrolled in various undergraduate and postgraduate degree programmes across the university, including engineering and information technology, communications, and business. In terms of content, I had decided to focus on the ways in which Australians engage with the natural environment, an area that provided a broad enough canvas to accommodate the various interests and backgrounds of my students and an area that coincided with my own political interests in environmental sustainability. In terms of process, I wanted each student to start their own research journey with a problem or puzzle that was particular and personal for them, something they were engaged in or saw in the news around them, something that pointed to an area of environmental interest that they could pursue as a small research project. I wanted to steer students away from more abstract issues such as climate change (how do we enter into such a large and complex debate?) or issues which have, unfortunately, become tired proxies for environmental concern, such as recycling. I wanted them to look at their immediate lives, to think about and interrogate their own intimate entanglement with the more-than-human world. I wanted to model that process of curiosity-led inquiry for my students. Modelling the process of research led me on a journey of oceanic engagement in the more-than-human world.

Where Am I in the More-Than-Human World?

Modelling the research process from 'where I am' is a good place to start if we take seriously the feminist principle that the everyday personal *is* political. So where am I, now? For me, one significant means of engagement with the environment has been through my own relationship with non-human animals, including my dog Sista (Appleby, 2012), from whom I learnt to be a vegetarian, and, more recently, marine animals encountered each day in my open water ocean swimming. Initially, when I began teaching this unit, my engagement was visceral and personal; I became aware that this personal engagement with animals sits alongside a rich and extensive history of feminist environmental scholarship and studies in critical human–animal relationships (see, for example, Haraway, 2003, 2008; Gruen, 1993; Noske, 1997; Plumwood, 1993).

From my personal human–animal perspective, I could have started my modelling of a research project with any number of everyday issues of importance to me, like the horrors of industrial factory farming and live animal exports, or the cruelty of horse and greyhound racing, or the exploitative overbreeding and sale of dogs as domestic pets. These were topics where I already had clear opinions about the (un)ethics of human–animal interactions, where my empathy for non-human animals was secure. But to start a research journey in an area where one already has a fixed opinion, a vision of the end point, is not the best place to start, because the authentic research journey depends on the vital driving force of curiosity and unknowing. In modelling a process of research, I wanted to go beyond my secure opinions and into a place of unsettlement, at the limit of my human–animal empathy, at the boundary of love and fear. Where was my own limit? That boundary was my relationship with sharks. An extract from my occasional swimming journal might give some idea of the ambivalence I feel in relation to these fellow travellers:

07:00, May 26, 2016. I'm swimming alone in open water, out from Manly beach. It's nearly winter and cold so I'm in my wetsuit, but the sky above is bright and with my goggles I can see through the clear water. I watch yellow tail, angel fish, old wives and mado swimming in pattery schools at various depths. Down further I see dusky whaler sharks cruising gracefully, there's been a lot of them this season. Almost a kilometer into the swim I sense someone swimming behind me, a flash of light on a moving body. I look underwater down the length of my own body, then turn to the side as I take a breath and then under water again as I breathe out. It's a shark, following me right up on the surface of the water. This is unusual, I've never been closely followed by a shark, and this one is right at my toes. Through the eye of the shark, do I look like kin, plaything, or like potential food? I take fright, stop and turn. When I face the shark it stops too. We are face to face in a moment of mutual regard, and time freezes. Then the shark turns to the east, out towards the horizon, and swims away. The shark and me, both swimming together in the ocean: I guess the shark, on seeing my face, lost interest in me. Yet the encounter remains a puzzlement.

Figure 2.1 Dusky Whaler Shark
Source: (photo Nick Dawkins)

As an ocean swimmer, every morning I swim between two of Sydney's northern beaches and I regularly encounter relatively harmless sharks who mostly appear to ignore my flapping along the ocean surface: wobbegongs, Port Jacksons, dusky whalers, and the occasional grey nurse. But saturating the everyday news media in 2014 and 2015 were other stories about fear-inducing shark encounters that made me uncertain about the human technologies such as netting, culling, tagging, and tracking designed to contain shark activity. During this time of increased media attention on fatal shark encounters, pro-shark rallies in Sydney and Perth campaigned against shark culling and even against the shark nets that hang off Sydney beaches. Were these people mad? Weren't the shark nets there to protect me against marauding great white sharks? Well, I wasn't sure, and it was *my un*ease over sharks and my ambivalence and uncertainty over the pro-shark movement that troubled and stretched my empathy for non-human animals. But it was this unease, and my own lack of understanding, that also motivated my own quest to know more about sharks and their place in the more-than-human world.

Sharks in the Human Imaginary

The entanglement of humans and sharks in the planetary environment stretches over space and time. For populations unfamiliar with coastal water-based activities, sharks might seem like the sort of animal that is remote from most people's experience. Yet shark bite incidents represent the most widely dispersed contact between humans and wildlife across the globe, 'from Cape Cod to Cape Town and Sydney to Sharm el Sheikh' (Neff, 2012, p. 89), and any place where ocean meets the land invites the meeting of sharks and humans. Sharks also tell us about deep time, and illuminate our fragile understanding of the natural world. Sharks precede humans by millions of evolutionary years, perfecting the art of embodied adaptation and survival over millennia.

In more recent time, sharks' teeth have helped humans understand more about deep time in Earth's formation, and more about our own miniscule temporal presence in planetary history. Until the mediaeval period, sharks' teeth found embedded in the ground in coastal areas were believed to be mystical objects with potent magical or healing powers. They were known as *glossopetrae*, a Latin word meaning 'tongue stones'. However, in 1666, a young Danish scientist, Neils Stensen, used a microscope to compare the structure of the glossopetrae with the teeth of a large white shark caught off the coast of Italy. He discovered that they were one and the same. Determined to discover why these fossilised shark teeth could be found in solid rocks located in inland areas far away from the sea, his studies led him to conclude that these areas must have at one time been under water before being covered by layers of sedimentary rock and lifted up to become dry land. His published dissertations gave scientific weight to the understanding that fossil records illustrated a geological history of life on Earth, and demonstrated the concept of deep time, in contradiction to Biblical notions of Earth's formation. With this entanglement, sharks' teeth came to symbolise the turning point between mediaeval and modern scientific ways of knowing the world (Owen, 2009).

Centuries later, scientific research confirms that sharks are crucial for healthy oceans and a healthy planet. Having evolved over 450 million years, compared to the appearance of humans only 200,000 years ago, sharks sit at the apex of the ocean's food chain. As Crawford (2008) argues, the shark's longevity on the planet is reason enough for their preservation: they are one of the oldest living vertebrate groups on the planet, older than the dinosaurs and our only living link to the Jurassic age. They are also among the longest-living vertebrates on the planet, with the Greenland shark, inhabiting icy Arctic waters, having a lifespan of between 300 and 500 years (Nielsen et al.,

2016), though the great white shark typically lives to the magical age of three score years and ten. It is not only the white sharks' lifespan that bears some uncanny and intriguing resemblances to humans. Sharks generally don't reach sexual maturity until they are in their teens, and compared to other fish, sharks have relatively few young, usually carried internally in the larger body of the female for between nine months and two years. There are over 450 shark species, leading largely solitary lives. Their activities keep marine life in balance, thereby protecting a complex ocean ecosystem that covers 70 per cent of the Earth's surface, supports the greatest biodiversity on the planet, removes half the world's greenhouse gasses, produces more oxygen than all rainforests combined, and controls the planet's climate and weather.

Now, in the Anthropocene, humans represent the only threat to the future existence of sharks, indirectly through habitat destruction, and directly through industrial fishing operations or targeted commercial shark finning operations that feed an appetite for shark fin soup. While sharks kill around a dozen humans in an average year, humans kill between 100 and 273 million sharks *every* year (Worm et al., 2013). An Infographic by Chernov and Ripetungi (2013, available at http://ripetungi.com/shark-attack/) provides a powerful representation of the extent of this slaughter. Because they are slow growing and have late reproductive maturity, such massive depletion of sharks exceeds the rebound rate for many shark populations, and the elimination of these apex predators has a catastrophic cascading effect not only on finely balanced ocean ecosystems but also in terms of disrupting the planet's carbon cycle, with negative consequences for climate change (Atwood et al., 2015). Around three-quarters of those killed are targeted for their fins (Clarke et al., 2006; Fields et al., 2017) and around one-third of the species identified in the fin trade are threatened with extinction (Fields et al., 2017). The high price of shark fins, over A$400 a kilogram (Elbra, 2012), means that the shark fin trade is widespread but difficult to accurately calculate and monitor. Although Australia has sole responsibility for the conservation of almost 25 per cent of the world's shark species (Allam, 2015), Australia also participates in the shark fin trade. Official data show that in 2015 Australia exported around 3400 kilograms of fins to Asia and also imported around 2340 kilograms, thereby sending mixed messages about Australia's commitments to environmental protection of endangered sharks (Australian Marine Conservation Society, 2017).

Shark, Culture, Language

The English language word 'shark' has a troubled history intertwined with the age of British imperial conquests and slave trading. Tracing various sources, Castro (2002) argues that 'shark' derives from the Mayan word 'xoc', and was introduced to England by seamen working for the sixteenth century Atlantic slave trader John Hawkins. In the present times, it is still the symbolic meanings attached to sharks, their representation in human language and culture, rather than their embodied physical impact, that most strongly influences popular perceptions and hampers progress in shark conservation. In a post-*Jaws* world, sharks can present an extreme embodiment of human fears: 'the shadow of the shark is the shadow of danger and death; the image of an ultimate evil . . . the inscrutability of a malign universe' (Tiffin, 2009, pp. 76–77). Symbolising this fear, the most persistent image that accompanies media discussion of sharks is that of the shark's head thrust through the ocean surface with gaping jaw and rows of pointed teeth. This metonymic image reproduces, with vicious circularity, a discursive notion that is readily recognised but largely independent of the living animal (Baker, 1993), and perpetuates the binary distinction between civilised human and barbaric, animal Other. Appearing, as they do, in the midst of our beachside summer holidays, sharks are said to represent a 'savage disruption to domestic calm', evoking the 'dangerous, unstable basis of life itself' and reminding us that the ocean remains 'one of the very few realms we have not yet totally conquered' (Tiffin, 2010, pp. 70–71).

Because a disproportionate fear has been coded into our relationship with sharks, public discourses in relation to sharks have been characterised by an indiscriminate and inaccurate use of the term 'shark attack' for any type of human–shark interaction. In the earlier days of white settlement in Australia, reports of shark bites referred to such interactions as 'accidents'. But by mid-20th century the concepts of the 'man-eater shark' and the 'rogue' shark with a 'taste for human flesh' had entered the language, portraying them as 'resident serial killers lurking in wait for human prey' (Neff & Hueter, 2013, p. 67). In contemporary media reports, sharks are described as 'lurking', 'prowling', 'stalking', 'menacing' and 'targeting' their human victims (Peace, 2015), and these metaphors of criminality in turn legitimise action-focused but ultimately ineffective retaliation policies such as government-sponsored hunting and killing expeditions (Gibbs & Warren, 2015). Such inept revenge activities pose significant problems for shark conservation, not only for the three shark species most often cited in media articles—great white shark, bull shark, and tiger shark—but also for harmless and endangered species such as the grey nurse (Muter et al., 2012).

Recognising the power of language in shaping our response to sharks, Neff and Hueter (2013) offer a proposal to alter the linguistic categorisation of human–shark incidents by replacing 'shark attack' with a more nuanced set of graded descriptors that include shark sightings, encounters, bites, and fatal bites. This linguistic modification is designed to 'decriminalize sharks in the mind of the public, and create a more objective understanding of the relationship between humans and sharks in the shared ocean spaces' (Neff & Hueter, 2013, p. 70). Yet it seems unlikely such objectivity, scientific rationalism, and linguistic cleansing would readily erase deep-seated, emotional human fear of sharks; and in any case, perhaps maintaining those fears about a lurking predator serves particular human interests for dominance and control of certain polities and places.

In many respects, language is central to the problematic ways in which we recognise, understand, and respond to all animals, not only sharks. Language has been controversially singled out as a sign of human exceptionalism and superiority over other animals (Derrida, 2008; Meijer, 2016) while simultaneously disregarding or underestimating the communicative arts of many species other than humans (Evans, 2014). Language is used as a means of separating humans from non-human animals, and presenting animal-Others as objects for human contemplation, exploitation, and consumption. Human language also limits our apprehension of animal Others who remain 'locked within our faulty representations of them' (Gruen & Weil, 2010, p. 480). This multistranded linguistic predicament at the heart of human–animal relationships has been addressed in recent years by a turn towards an embodied and affective way of relating to human engagement in the world around us. This is a form of engagement that seeks to retrieve a 'relational experience of being' amongst human- and non-human animals 'that is outside the bounds of language and the meanings it imposes and enables' (Gruen & Weil, 2012, p. 481).

Sharks in the Australian Imaginary

Australians have a particularly strong relationship with sharks. Rock carvings around the Sydney area illustrate the long, complex, Indigenous tradition of human–shark interaction that stretches back thousands of years and extends up to the present day. Around the Australian coast and into the Torres Strait to the north, sharks have been an important part of the cultural and spiritual life of Indigenous saltwater people: the shark is a totem, a source of food, a guardian of coastal habitats, a symbol of strength and justice, a source of inspiration and motivation (Allam, 2015).

The schism between Indigenous and settler Australian relationships with sharks is crystalised in the written compendium of fatal shark attacks in Australia. The first recorded incident cites an Aboriginal child who told early European colonists that his mother had been 'bitten in two by a shark' in Sydney's Port Jackson (Tench, 1793). Sadly, and perhaps unsurprisingly, in this written account recorded just a few years after the arrival of convicts from Britain, the human victim is nameless, evoking in this silence the invaders' notion of the Australian continent as an empty land, a *terra nullius*, open, and available for conquest.

Even before British colonial invasion, the English language marked the land when, in 1699, English pirate and navigator William Dampier reached the western coast of New Holland (Australia) where he recorded detailed observations of wildlife and named the place of his landfall 'Shark Bay' due to the abundance of these creatures in the surrounding waters. In this sense, the process of naming the world with English language became entangled with the body of the shark in the white 'discovery' of Australia during the British imperial mission. As Sturma (1986) wryly observes, such reports of a land surrounded by oceanic predators may have had a certain appeal to British governments when selecting a place to create a penal colony to accommodate an overflow of convicted criminals in England. For these Europeans, the shark was an instrument and symbol of death, and about 20 fatal attacks were recorded during the first century of British colonisation.

From the turn of the 20th century to the present day the incidence of human–shark interactions has increased in line with the expansion of human populations in coastal areas and the growing popularity of water-based recreation activities (West, 2011). Yet since 2000 there have been on average only two human fatalities per year, a remarkably small number especially when compared with other causes of death, for example by drowning or road accident. Indeed, roughly the same number of people died by drowning in a single year—271 fatalities from July 2014 to June 2015—as those that have died as a result of shark encounters in all the years since the arrival of European colonists in 1788. Yet for many non-Indigenous occupants on this continent the notion of sharks as potential predators and humans as potential prey continues to invoke postcolonial anxieties over white Australian notions of belonging in a hostile foreign land (Simpson, 2010) and in a surrounding ocean that breeds sharks who are emblematic of nature in its most violent and vicious form (Peace, 2015). It has been said that sharks are part of Australia's international mystique (Sturma, 1986) and even the official recording of proceedings in our premier state parliament notes that 'the shark, and fear of shark attack, has a special place in the Australian psyche' (cited in Neff, 2012, p. 99).

The meanings attached to sharks in Australia and elsewhere frequently carry a particular gendered and sexualised subtext. In Australia, the idea that men have the fearless courage to fight sharks is part of our macho culture and an element in 'the last frontier complex' (Tiffin, 2010, p. 69). Male triumphalism both here and in the USA has been a component of shark hunting and characterises countless photographs of fishermen proudly posing beside a dead shark hung ignominiously by its tail (Tiffin, 2010). According to Tiffin, Australians' outwardly casual approach to sharks further bolsters a sense of masculine bravado and risk-taking; yet when sharks do bite a surfer or diver (most often male and white), Australian attitudes and responses differ little from those generally expressed in other Western cultures. Such an affront to masculinity is regularly met with public calls for shark culling, beach netting, and aerial surveillance. Nevertheless, a marked shift towards more positive human responses to sharks has been evident in recent years.

Changing Human–Shark Relationships

This shift can be seen in media accounts of human–shark interactions, where sensational images and text describing shark 'attacks' is now more often interspersed with stories that highlight the responsibilities of humans and the environmental significance of sharks. While modest, such inclusions indicate an increasing public appreciation of sharks, shark science, and conservation (see, for example, media studies by Boissonneault et al., 2005; Muter et al., 2012; Whatmough, Van Putten & Chin, 2011) and can potentially function as a form of shared public pedagogy. More broadly, these new, nuanced forms of representation and response seem to point towards an emerging ethic that encompasses a more complex and dynamic set of interrelationships between humans and other animals (Simpson, 2010). This dynamic representational complexity can be seen in the diverse reports of an encounter between Australian champion surfer, Mick Fanning, and a great white shark during a World Surfing League competition in South Africa (discussed in more detail in Chapter 4). In the following account, I describe the discursive shifts evident in reports of a less well-known incident that occurred at my local swimming beach several months ago.

On September 11, 2017 a great white shark washed up at midday on Manly beach, one of the most popular swimming and surfing locations in Australia. Onlookers moved the shark to the nearby ocean pool at Fairy Bower. Half a world away in Britain, a sequence of online newspaper reports of the incident, described in more detail below, illustrate a remarkable turn over a single day in media representations of the shark who was linguistically transfigured from a lurking predator to a loveable baby called Fluffy. The media also revised its account of human responses to the same shark from 'terrified' and 'stunned' to a show of 'heart-warming' curiosity and care.

At 05:41 (GMT) on 11 September, the online site of UK-based tabloid the *Daily Mail* ran an initial version of the story under the extended headline 'Terrified swimmers flee the water at Sydney's Manly beach after a GREAT WHITE SHARK washes up on shore—before do-gooders release the predator into a nearby ocean pool' (Morgan, 2017a). In this version, the scene was 'dramatic', the 'dangerous', 'predatory animal' was 'rapidly moving its tail on the shores of Manly Beach' while 'terrified beachgoers were forced to flee'. Once the shark was moved it was reported to be 'lurking in the shallow rock pool waters as stunned sunbathers watched on'. The accompanying photos showed a contradictory image: on the left, the photographic image of a shark stranded on sand; and on the right, an image of the shark in a rock pool beside which two bikini-clad sunbathers appear in relaxed poses, one lying prone and watching the shark swimming nearby in the water, another sitting up, toes dangling over the edge of the pool and looking at her mobile phone. Within this article was a second, separate report of an incident that occurred some hours earlier when a surfer further north on the east coast was 'rushed to hospital after an apparent shark attack left him bleeding and his board snapped'. This second part of the story was illustrated with close-up photos of the gash in the surfer's thigh, visible through a tear in the man's wetsuit, and the surfboard snapped in two.

This initial report of the shark incident at Manly displays stereotypical discourses in which terrified beachgoers (potential victims) escape from a dangerous, predatory animal. Humans who attempt to save the shark are described in pejorative terms as 'do-gooders', and beachgoers or surfers who venture into the ocean (like the north-coast surfer) are vulnerable to vicious attacks. The accompanying images of a stranded shark, and of young women sunbathing nonchalantly beside the shark, present two discourses that contradict the written account: discourses of shark-as-vulnerable, and human–animal amicable coexistence. It's as if the writer cannot relinquish the traditional discourse of shark as monster, despite the visible evidence.

Within minutes this discursive discordance showed signs of resolution as the rapidly evolving online headlines began to change. The first video of the event, posted at 05:49 (GMT) was accompanied by a more subdued headline, with no mention of terrified swimmers, do-gooders, or lurking predators: 'Beached shark at Sydney's Manly Beach rescued and put in pool'. The discursive representation of the shark had shifted: the shark was now described as worthy of rescue, with phrases more often used to refer to the sympathy-inducing beached whales that are the target of rescue activities when they appear on Australian beaches. By 07:25 (GMT) the text accompanying the next video reported that 'Beachgoers were amazed to see a great white shark swimming in popular Manly pool': clearly, no longer terrified.

By 11:21 (GMT) the next full article in the *Daily Mail* displayed a further shift in this sympathetic direction, appearing under the headline 'Great white shark called Fluffy who sent families fleeing in terror after washing up on Sydney's Manly beach to be released back into the wild after spending the night at an aquarium' (Morgan, 2017b). The story primarily focussed on how the shark, now with the 'nickname' Fluffy, and referred to as 'he', was cared for overnight by 'marine experts' from a local aquarium and prepared for release into the open ocean: 'the shark is better suited to recovery out in its [own] environment'. The shark was reported to have 'superficial injuries' and had become 'a bit tired and exhausted and then stressed with the waves and all the people around it'.

Then, at 11:35 (GMT) the *Daily Mail* reported on 'The heart-warming moment Sydney's favourite shark is released back into the wild after being rescued and spending the night in an aquarium' (Morgan, 2017c). The shark has now been re-storied as a victim, eliciting unalloyed sympathy from Sydney humans, and leaving humans in the role of humble heroes in an unlikely environmental rescue event. The shark appeared to be 'in healthy condition' and experts were 'optimistic about its survival': 'It was truly a privilege to work with this species and it is always great to be able to release an animal like this back to the wild and to see the amount of public support he had'. The marine expert had chosen the name Fluffy to help 'combat the bad image of sharks', an image that is nevertheless retained by linguistic traces in this version of the body of the story. Words such as 'thrashing' and 'scary' remain, so that the earlier discourse of sharks as monsters has not been fully expunged. The trace of the monster remains embedded in the revised narrative of amateur and expert care for Fluffy, and the lauded human actions aimed at releasing the shark to freedom in his open water habitat. These competing discourses of terror and care sit uncomfortably entangled, side-by-side, with each continually emerging and subsiding, but never completely disappearing.

Finally, at 16:31pm an AFP report in the *Daily Mail* ('Fluffy the great white shark', 2017) announced that Fluffy was heading 'back to sea' after 'spending the night in an aquarium'. In this concluding account, 'Fluffy' was described in diminutive terms as a 'baby great white shark', its size reduced to just 1.5 metres. In one short day, the shark had shifted from a figure of terror to a creature deserving of heart-warming affection and protection.

Meanwhile, the local Northern Beaches newspaper, *The Manly Daily*, consistently reported the event in language that foregrounded the flurry of positive human excitement raised by the shark's appearance on the beach. From the outset the local newspaper focussed on the popularity of the shark and the extent to which it attracted people's curiosity and desire: instead of 'forcing' humans to 'flee' in 'terror', the shark had, in this version, drawn crowds towards its charismatic embodied presence. In the first print version, a benign headline, 'Shark washes up at Manly', was followed by the subheading 'Crowds flock to Fairy Bower pool to catch a glimpse of ocean predator as it recovers' (Kay & Lowe, 2017). The lead paragraph then opens with an account of 'amazed onlookers [who] gathered' to see an 'injured great white shark lying on a popular Manly beach' and is illustrated with a photo of a girl dressed in school uniform, holding up a mobile phone and bending over the edge of the pool to photograph the shark. The report then focussed on the marine experts' rescue efforts, observations of the shark's 'threatened species' status, and descriptions of excited 'daredevil spectators [who] were seen jumping into the pool for a once-in-a-lifetime chance to swim with the ocean predator'. In this report, it seems the discourse of threat lingers with the word 'predator', but only as a magnetic motivating force for human desire and benevolent action.

By the following day, the *Manly Daily* had shifted its focus to a video recording that captured the unsuccessful attempt by a local tradesman to drag the beached shark back into the sea. This parallel narrative, under the headline 'Incredible twist to tail', blends several key concepts that shape the 'Aussie hero' discourse by describing 'the moment a "quintessential" Aussie bloke strips down to his undies at Manly Beach before boldly trying to save the life of an injured great white shark' (Kay, 2017). This is the discourse of the everyday Aussie bloke who fearlessly tackles a notorious monster, a familiar trope instantiated in figures such as the fictional Crocodile Dundee and the late Steve Irwin. The newspaper account also articulates a related discourse of casual nonchalance supposedly adopted by (mostly male) Australians—often for the benefit of outsiders—in response to our 'deadly' creatures, a characteristic observed by travel writer Bill Bryson (2000) in his account of swimming at Manly beach. Finally, a third discourse of humble modesty serves to complete the Aussie hero image, as the 'tradie' who waded into the water 'to try to help the distressed animal' is quoted as saying: 'I think he was that worn out and stressed that I don't think he would have even tried to have a nibble. It was just a young bloke looking for a hand.... Everyone thinks I'm a legend but I don't think so... I was just really doing what needed to be done'. In this account, the shark has become a helpless victim waiting to be rescued, in an act of mateship, by the humble, heroic Aussie male.

The earlier discourse of a terrorising great white shark juxtaposed with a relatively benign account of the stranded shark in need of rescue is typical of a complex and conflicted response to the figure and body of the shark in contemporary Australian culture. In recent years, we have seen diverse signs of this shifting discursive representation mixed with continuing signs of the threat that great white sharks still pose to ocean-going humans. In 2013, 'No Shark Cull' rallies were publicised on social media and drew large crowds on Manly Beach and across the nation. The rallies, where protesters displayed placards with environmental messages such as 'Healthy oceans need sharks' were mounted in opposition to government measures to control sharks by baiting and culling. As mentioned at the outset, these were the rallies that served to motivate my own investigations into human relationships with sharks. In subsequent years, the No Shark Cull movement has worked to raise awareness about the ecological importance of sharks and to educate the public on the environmental dangers posed by the measures used to eliminate sharks from our coastal waters. Calls for shark culling continue to surface in the wake of any fatal shark bites but the public and institutional responses have changed: culling is now more often rejected as a control measure on the basis that there is no evidence that it actually makes our beaches safer (Laschon, 2017) and environmental sustainability discourses now counter the discourses of fear. It seems efforts towards public education have had a positive effect.

In a further sign of these shifting times, 2016 saw the closure of the iconic vintage 'Shark Show' in Queensland, an exhibition that comprised a series of installations that patrons entered through the gaping jaws of a shark (Leigo & Adcock, 2016). The Shark Show was owned by notorious shark hunter Vic Hislop, who caught sharks for the equally notorious artist Damien Hirst (discussed in more detail in Chapter 3). The Shark Show traded on displays that demonised the shark, but the tide of public opinion has clearly changed over recent decades and an appetite for conservation has gradually emerged to challenge and complicate the ignorance and fear that nevertheless lingers, just under the surface.

After Fluffy

After Fluffy's appearance in September, and into the summer of 2017–2018, I continued to swim out into the ocean from Manly beach, regardless of the arrival of the unfortunate great white shark. Not through bravado (after all, I tend to stay out of the water if there's stinging bluebottles or jimbles), but simply because the chance of any dangerous mishap with a shark seems so unimaginably remote. Despite Australia's notoriety as the nation recording the most fatalities as a consequence of shark bites in recent years, there has been no fatal encounter with a shark on Sydney's ocean beaches since 1936 (though there have been more recent incidents in Sydney's other waterways). However, oft-quoted statistics regarding the rarity of shark attacks never quite manage to totally expel those submerged fears that can resurface whenever a shark bumps or bites a human.

At the same time, there is an irresistible urge incited by the shark that speaks to a deep unconscious desire in humans. Given the extent to which these animals have been subjected to material and discursive domination by humans, there is something remarkable, exciting, liberating, awe-inspiring in the continuing power they exercise over the human imagination. They

Figure 2.2 Kissing the Shark at No Shark Cull Rally

Source: (photo David Jenkins—Whale Spotter)

Figure 2.3 Swimming With Sharks
Source: (photo Elaine de Jager)

evade, they resist, and sometimes they dominate humans. Swimming with a solitary shark, it's her exercise of power that attracts me. If an earlier era of ecofeminist arguments revolved around the notion of alignment across oppressions of women, animals, and all Others, perhaps the shark invites us to move on from that place of oppression and refocus on a more powerful agentive experience of survival and freedom.

3   Shark Arts

The white naked body of a woman is turned towards the viewer. Her arms
are chained to a rock by the sea, her face shows fear. In the sea is a thrashing
monstrous form, an animal with gaping jaws. In the sky above a male figure
brandishing a sword swoops down to attack the sea monster. These three figures come together in countless renditions of Perseus rescuing Andromeda
from her fate: to be ravished by Cetus, the monster in the sea. A dynamic
interpretation of this fertile narrative is presented in Titian's 16th century
painting *Perseus and Andromeda* (1554–1556).[1]
     This chapter offers a selective survey of the ways in which sharks, as
iconic sea creatures, have been used in the visual arts in ways that have frequently served to reproduce and amplify traditional notions of human masculinity, femininity, and normative heterosexuality. Sea monsters and shark
images from the classical and romantic period of Western art will appear,
along with shark sculptures, installations, and performances from contemporary Western and Australian Indigenous arts. Through this discussion, I
suggest that despite the ubiquity of human–shark representations that serve
to bolster heteronormativity, resistant readings of human–shark interactions
are also possible. These offer a means of imagining and enacting more positive relationships amongst humans and between humans and other animals.

Andromeda and the Sea Monster

In the original Greek narrative, Andromeda is the beautiful daughter of King
Cepheus and Queen Cassiopeia of Aethiopia. Queen Cassiopeia claimed
that her daughter Andromeda was more beautiful than the Nereids, or sea
nymphs, thereby infuriating Poseidon, god of the sea. In revenge, Poseidon
sent Cetus the sea monster to ravage Aethiopia. As a sacrifice to appease the
monster, Andromeda was chained to a rock next to the sea but was rescued
by Perseus, the son of Zeus, who slayed the beast and married Andromeda.
From a contemporary perspective, the Andromeda myth is an archetype of

the 'princess and dragon' motif in which the passive female figure is rescued from the vicious beast by the daring actions of a male hero.

The Andromeda myth provided inspiration for numerous artists during the European Renaissance and Baroque periods, and most renditions capture the moment when the three main characters—Perseus, Andromeda, and the monster—come together with the focus clearly on the naked and chained body of the sacrificial heroine. She is the central object of our vision: positioned in the foreground, larger than the other figures, naked, and dazzlingly white. Titian's painting *Perseus and Andromeda* (1554–1556) illustrates the point advanced by John Berger (1972) over four decades ago that in traditional European art 'men act and women appear' (p. 45), and that female nudes reflect submission to the male viewer as 'the owner of both woman and painting' (p. 52). Where Andromeda is the passive object, Perseus is the male hero and man of action who propels the narrative forward. He is depicted hurtling downwards from the heavenly realm towards monstrous Cetus who arches upwards, defensively, from the turbid sea. The man and beast fight for the body of the naked female. In this sense, the sea monster also provides the motivation for a display of patriarchal power and gender hierarchies, the rationale for a display of action-oriented hero masculinity and a weak, to-be-rescued femininity.

What, then, can we say about the figure and role of Cetus, the sea monster? The sea monster is a figure of horror from the deep, from an obscure domain beyond the edge of knowledge, from the uncharted watery regions beyond the mapped world, from the abyss, from the unconscious, a figure of horror and fear. The sea monster is the Other, the unspeakable, bestial dark side of humanity. And, in ancient lore, the sea monster is also female: the primordial mother, goddess, creator, and destroyer. In this case, is the sea goddess about to devour Andromeda or are Andromeda and the terrifying sea goddess–monster already one and the same, twin manifestations of female power? For Graves (1961) and Caputi (1978), who trace the origin of the myth to the tumultuous historical transition from an earlier matriarchal society to a patriarchal, agrarian society, the female sea monster is the materialised emanation of Andromeda, her human female body chained to the rock by Perseus in order to prevent her from interfering with his struggle to slay her own monstrous oceanic incarnation.

By the 18th century, the age of European navigation, exploration, and exploitation of the world, the mythical sea monster had evolved into the naturalistic form of the shark that we recognise today. A figure approximating this form appears in a widely discussed painting from the 18th century, John Singleton Copley's painting *Watson and the Shark* (1778), which depicts the fateful encounter between 14-year-old Watson and a shark in Cuba's Havana Harbour in 1749.[2] This was an era marked by American revolt against British colonial power, by increasing protest against the trans-atlantic slave trade, and by Euro–American conquest of a new oceanic and terrestrial wilderness. Copley's painting shows a naked and distressed white figure in the water, stretched horizontally along the lower left of the canvas, the shark approaching along the lower right with jaws open in the direction of the swimmer and outwards towards the viewer, and a group of nine men in a boat above these two, arranged in various postures ready to rescue the victim from the shark's open jaws.

Analyses of the painting have focussed on its religious and political symbolism, which is variously said to represent salvation and resurrection, or the struggle for American freedom from the jaws of British rule. Others have focussed on the work's appropriation of classical composition in which key authority figures are traditionally placed at the apex of a triangle, with animals and slave at the base. Such analyses have argued about the historical significance of Copley's unorthodox inversion which places the figure of a black man near the apex of the group, and a white victim (together with the shark) at the base. But whether Copley's image represents a conservative or liberatory vision of racial hierarchies is unclear (Boime, 1989; Masur, 1994).

From my perspective, the highest point in the compositional pyramid appears to be occupied by the harpoon-like boathook that is launched by the brightly illuminated white hero standing erect on the right side of the composition. The harpoon is thrust diagonally downwards, towards the shark. The whole movement of the painting, including the white outstretched arm of the victim below, sweeps upwards towards this heroic figure. In this respect Copley's harpoon-thrusting hero replicates the action of Perseus brandishing his sword ready to destroy the sea monster, while the naked white figure in the watery foreground, waiting to be rescued, takes the place of Andromeda as the female victim. Thus, although Copley's historical painting has shifted the subject matter from a traditional setting in antiquity towards a more contemporary rendition depicting events involving the 'common man', the most potent force in the composition remains condensed in the virile figure of the white action hero directed towards destroying the ocean monster in the form of the shark.

As art historians have pointed out, the painting remains something of a mystery even today, despite the volumes written about its possible meanings (Clancy, 2012; Masur, 1994). Indeed, Masur (1994, p. 430) argues that 'perhaps no other painting by an American artist has received so much critical attention' and been the object of such intense debate and diverse interpretations.

I take this ongoing debate over interpretation as an invitation to offer my own reading of Copley's image. In first viewing the painting, with no prior knowledge of the historical event that it depicts, I saw the floating white figure in the water as that of a woman: in luminous white, a flailing twisted body exposing the breasts and modestly hiding the genitals, a single arm outstretched in pleading, and with long blonde hair floating in the water. This is not a figure of heroic combat, but a vulnerable, white, naked body, displayed in its purity, virtue, and helplessness. What the figure recalled, for me, was the same struggling naked female figures I remembered in a painting from my days as a student of art history: these were the figures in Peter Paul Rubens' *The Rape of the Daughters of Leucippus* (1615–1618).[3]

The subject of Rubens' painting returns us to Greek mythology, depicting twin brothers Castor and Pollux abducting two sisters Phoebe and Hilaeira. As Carroll (1989) observes, *The Rape* offers an allegorical conflation of political, territorial, and sexual conquest in 16th century Europe and 'a celebratory depiction of sexual violence and of the forcible subjugation of women by men' (p. 3). For a young art history student in the 1970s, this was a discomforting image of female struggle. Transposed onto the body of Watson, I saw the pale, twisted figure in the water as a feminine sacrifice about to be swallowed by the marauding shark, or to be pulled into a boat full of male figures.

Once the historical identity of Watson as a *boy* in the painting is known, alternative readings and implications are possible. At the time Copley was commissioned by Brook Watson to paint the depicted event, Watson had become a successful merchant and was hoping to boost his public standing and garner support for his aspirations to political office in England. Watson's goal was achieved with the exhibition of Copley's painting, which celebrated the boyhood incident in which Watson's right foot was bitten and maimed by the shark, resulting in the amputation of his lower leg:

> The picture stood as a powerful agent of propaganda for [Watson] the aspiring businessman, a visual discourse attesting to the great depths from which he rose before reaching his current station. It was a persuasive rhetoric, one strategically contracted to co-opt the self-serving ambitions of its subject and carpet his way to political victory.
>
> (Ashton, 2009, p. 18)

Critical interpretations of the painting have suggested that Copley's composition draws not only on the specific event of the shark attack, but on various sources depicted in classical myths, biblical stories, or historical movements, and it is notable that each of these entails dramatic actions involving all-male actors, including ancient warriors, priests, prophets, the disciples of Christ, American insurgents, and Atlantic seafarers, merchants, and slave traders (Clancy, 2012; Jaffe, 1977; Masur, 1994; Torres,

2016). Each source, and Copley's acclaimed painting, also implicitly asks profound questions about the struggle between man and a powerful, unpredictable natural world represented by the treacherous ocean and the shark as voracious sea monster. But whether the struggle is undertaken and resolved through human agency or divine intervention, it seems to be, in all accounts, a struggle of masculinity centring the activities of men, and 'appealing to the common man' as a representative for universal human experience (Masur, 1994, p. 442). Enhancing that manly purpose, through binary contrast, is the 'ultimate *otherness* of the animal' (Aloi, 2011, p. xvi) in the image of the reviled shark.

Embalming the Shark

In 1991, advertising magnate and art collector Charles Saatchi provided £50,000 for Damien Hirst to produce a taxidermied shark as a work of art.[4] The shark, pickled in formaldehyde and displayed in a steel and glass tank, became an infamous icon of the contemporary art scene in Britain and helped to promote Hirst's career as the leading *enfant terrible* of the so-called Young British Artists. Hirst's habit was to confront audiences with symbols of mortality, displayed through the dead bodies of once-living animals, including a lamb, a dog, and a rotting cow's head. The animals were killed in order to make sensational and saleable 'art', and with this tactic Hirst was on his way to becoming one of the wealthiest individuals in the UK and the world's wealthiest living artist (Vogel, 2006). The original £50,000 figure paid to produce the pickled shark was intended by Hirst to be an 'outrageous price, set as much for the publicity it would attract as for the monetary return' (Thompson, 2008, p. 70).

The four-metre tiger shark displayed in the glass tank was one of several caught by notorious Australian shark hunter Vic Hislop at Hirst's behest. It had been captured and killed off the Australian coastline, and then transported to Britain in a freezer compartment. Hirst's title for this installation, *The Physical Impossibility of Death in the Mind of Someone Living* (and sometimes simply referred to as *The Shark*) indicates his intention to confront the viewer and invoke an existential fear of mortality. In a magazine interview, Hirst explained his motivations and meaning: 'I like the idea of a thing to describe a feeling. A shark is frightening, bigger than you are, in an environment unknown to you. It looks alive when it's dead and dead when it's alive' (cited in Thompson, 2008, p. 70). In this sense, *The Shark* is intended to evoke a 'sense of impotence experienced in front of a potentially deadly force of nature' (Aloi, 2011, p. 4). But encased in its glass box, the illusion of the shark's potent liveliness began to fade as the specimen gradually decomposed: its skin grew wrinkled, the body sagged, a fin fell off, and the tank turned murky. In 1993, Saatchi's curators finally had the shark skinned then stretched over a weighted fibreglass mould.

With a new $12 million price tag, the shark was to be purchased in 2004 by USA hedge fund billionaire Steve Cohen, who subsequently paid Hirst to revive the artwork. Hirst arranged for five more sharks to be caught, killed, and imported from Australian waters, each one to eventually be pickled, boxed, and sold for millions of dollars to art collectors. One of the sharks sent to Hirst was a great white, a protected species, so killing and removing it from Australian waters was controversial. Undeterred by such bureaucratic rulings, Hirst's representatives took care of all the paperwork (Crabb, 2006). The particular tiger shark chosen to replace Cohen's model was a middle-aged female, about 25 to 30 years old, and her body was filled with, and bathed in, 224 gallons of poisonous formaldehyde (Vogel, 2006). Perhaps unsurprisingly, responses to Hirst's taxidermied animals have often been harsh. Gene Ray's (2004, p. 129) blistering critique of Hirst's installation of dead flies and rotting cow's head could equally be applied to the shark: the animal's misery is not represented, but is instead cynically and barbarously actualised, so that 'Art's old howl of protest ends here in a snigger and a shrug'.

In my reading of Hirst's shark, three interrelated discourses emerge. The first is to do with the entanglement of masculinities in the globalised finance and art industries in which the shark's body is a traded commodity. Thompson's (2008) detailed description of the 2004 auction for the shark presents a crowd of greedy men, a welter of hegemonic masculinities at the zenith of the sub-prime fiasco: the wealthy artist selling to a global market of hyper-rich speculators; the advertising guru and collector from London, then centre of the financial world; the famous New York–based art dealer; the director of London's Tate Modern; the American hedge fund manager; and, lurking in the background, the Australian shark hunter. The auction scrum, motivated by the prospect of speculative financial gain, is a microcosm of the shark's new world, one in which contemporary art had been consumed and corrupted by globalised, unregulated, high finance (Harris, 2013). Of course, art and finance have always been closely linked, but from the late 20th century this relationship had become particularly explicit with the monetisation and marketing of contemporary art, 'embracing of the language and tactics of the markets and financial engineering' (Harris, 2013, p. 30). Given the enormous celebrity and profits that Hirst has reaped from his dead sharks, I'm persuaded by White's (2013, para 18) argument that the figure of the shark, in human language a symbol for predatory capitalism, serves here as 'an image of nature being not only hostile, but as rapacious, insatiable, and unfeeling as capital accumulation itself'.

The second discourse emerges from the way the body of the shark in its glass case echoes an earlier age of European imperialism. For me the poor pickled shark speaks of a colonial past when exotic exhibits from the far outposts such as *Terra Australis* were captured, boxed up as curious objects, transported to the imperial centre, and displayed as a spectacle for the entertainment of an English public. In the present day, Hirst's shark is both his exotic specimen and his personal trophy, slaughtered, and stuffed at his command, to be read as 'a masculine statement of power addressing the art world at large' (Aloi, 2011, p. 5). For those of us swimming amongst living sharks in the Antipodes, Hirst's patriarchal, colonising display fails to come to grips with either the reality and embodied sensuality of swimming with sharks as fellow earthlings, or with the broader entanglement of humans in a more-than-human world.

The third discourse, closely related to the second, is one that concerns the body of the sentient animal as a commodity: a living being to be captured, slaughtered, shipped, stuffed, and traded for human purposes. The practice of taxidermy which emerged in the 18th century coincided with the deepening divisions between nature and culture wrought by the industrial revolution, and has been revived in animal art over recent decades, especially in the form of 'botched taxidermy' (Baker, 2000). In its Victorian iteration, taxidermy was a practice of containment, the production of a subjugated wilderness, a process of animal translation from subject-being to object-being, resulting in something that never in fact existed (Aloi, 2011). The taxidermied animal from the colonies was designed to represent, on the one hand, 'tangible proof of the greatness of nature' and 'the manifestation of the subjugation of nature that man alone is capable of', while at the same time providing a map of imperial ownership (Aloi, 2011, p. 27). In this sense, the taxidermied object, like the photograph, can be read through Roland Barthes' (1982, p. 91) argument: it is not a memory of the real, but it 'actually blocks memory, quickly becomes a counter-memory'. Or in Baudrillard's terms, we might view *The Shark* as a copy without an original.

The hunting of large aggressive animals for museum display in the 18th and 19th centuries was purportedly undertaken in the name of science and education, but was also motivated by individual hunters' 'hunger for the trophy' and desire to demonstrate an act of manly heroism. In the present day, Hirst has outsourced the shark hunt and kill to the Australian fisherman, but nevertheless glories in the dead shark body as trophy. The shark has been stripped of its individual history, deterritorialised, reduced to a generic species representative, suspended in its glass box, labelled with a fixed, predetermined meaning, left to decay as a sad reminder of a life cut short. While the use of 'botched taxidermy' in postmodern art has produced unexpected works that 'encourage open and imaginative thought' rather than 'banally symbolizing things already known' (Baker, 2000, pp. 61–62), Hirst's *Shark*, as a deeply conservative display of traditional discourses, unfortunately fails in this regard.

In his curiously approving analysis of Hirst's *Shark*, Steve Baker (2000, p. 98) argues that 'part of what postmodern art may be able to do with the animal is to take both it and the viewer out of their familiar meaning-laden contexts'. He goes on to quote from a television interview in which Hirst claimed that when the viewer gets close enough to the shark, 'you get a feeling of what it would be like to be in the water with it. . . . Being in water with a shark you're out of your element' (cited in Baker, 2000, p. 98). But surely this statement could only be made by a land-living human, someone who doesn't swim with all sorts of sharks and fish, someone for whom the oceanic world remains implacably foreign.

Grammatically, I read Hirst's *Shark* not as an opening question, but as a closed statement. In the exploitation and containment of the animal, and in the labelling designed to direct audience responses to feelings of fear, Hirst restates an age-old metaphor, a tired anthropocentric 'truth', and reiterates a broader received wisdom about human mastery over other creatures. If I read Hirst's work literally, I read the body of a living animal killed for human pleasure and profit; if I read the statement metaphorically as death, I see a meaning that is remarkably unimaginative, a meaning where the shark remains as the monstrous Other, kept firmly in a bounded box (literally and metaphorically) outside of—separated from— the human subject. Hirst as Midas: taking the body of the living shark and turning it to personal profit. There seems to be little evidence of questioning or curiosity or openness to the unknown, let alone a will for change in historical hierarchies, nothing beyond the quest for reinstating traditional, privileged, white masculine power.

Painting With *Shark Bite*

At around the same time that Hirst was working on the bodies of dead sharks, two other British artists, Olly Williams and Suzi Winstanley (www. ollysuzi.com), were developing a very different practice of human engagement with the world of other animals. Describing themselves as passionate conservationists, Olly and Suzi's collaborative work takes the form of paintings and drawings that reflect their immediate encounters and interactions with wild animals, often endangered predators, in their natural habitat, including great white sharks in the ocean off South Africa. For these shark encounters, Olly, and Suzi worked in a small flimsy cage lowered into the ocean around which swam more than thirty sharks. Their paintings use both conventional and natural materials, including natural dyes, sap, blood, and soil, and the animals with whom they collaborate are 'encouraged, without manipulation or coercion, to interact with the work and mark it further themselves' (Baker, 2000, p. 12). In each case the entire process is documented as a performance by their collaborating photographer, Greg Williams. One of the resulting photographic images, *Shark Bite*[5] (1997) captures the moment when an individual shark is about to take a bite from Olly and Suzi's painting as it floats in the ocean. In this performance, the bitten fragment was then spat out and retrieved. Disorderly, haphazard, unpredictable; and yet, as an experiential performance, the work can be read as a mark of the intimate ecological interactions and interdependences of humans and other animals in the contemporary world: 'a reminder of the limits of human understanding and influence, but also of the value of working *at those limits*' (Baker, 2000, p. 16).

Although Olly and Suzi had initially experienced the usual cultural associations of fear associated with the movie *Jaws*, they had, unlike Hirst, chosen to interact personally with the sharks in their ocean habitat. In doing so, along with their fear the artists became intimately aware of the shark's form and beauty: 'you see it buoyed up in its own environment, and there it's perfection' (Olly, cited in Baker, 2000, p. 132). In their temporary and precarious oceanic alliance with the sharks, the artists look at the animal, the animal looks back. There is fear on the humans' side, but also curiosity on both sides, in evidence as the sharks swim up to the cage and veer away at the last moment. Olly and Suzi's *Shark Bite* resists pre-given meanings of human mastery and domination over other animals, and of sharks as containable, reduced to a fixed and predictable representation in human discourse. Instead of taking up the position of the all-knowing individual, author, and hero, the artists work collaboratively with each other, painting hand-over-hand, and in a creative engagement with living animals.

How can we think about the place of language in relation to the work of Olly and Suzi and the shark? First, their images are in some ways akin to a record of spoken language. Their website states that 'for the last 30 years we've been in a conversation with the natural world' (ollysuzi.com). They work in the moment, rushed, in urgency, to capture the fleeting appearance of the animal, the here-and-now immediacy of the body in living motion in the wild. Certainly there is a degree of preparation, staging, expectation, in the performance, and then in selection and editing for exhibition. But there is also, crucially, the primary element of engagement in happening, in the unexpected, the ephemeral and transient. Their work captures not only the immediacy of the shark in that brief second of interaction, but also their own embodied experience of being there 'in five metres of choppy swell in a crappy cage with each other banging around and this thing trying to eat us.

That's our interpretation of what's real and beautiful' (Olly, cited in Baker, 2013, p. 32).

Shark Bite is both the record of an engagement with the shark and a record of the emergent, multimodal language that arises in the contact zone of that engagement. The shark and humans come together in an oceanic contact zone; the shark approaches the humans' cage then the shark swims away; the artists observe the shark, paint; the painting is offered to the shark; the shark bites the painting and spits out the bitten scrap. Humans and shark each make marks in the contact zone, with the marks comprising a 'pidgin language', 'chaotic, barbarous, lacking in structure' (Pratt, 1992, p. 6). Taking up the notion of a new, embodied contact language, Olly and Suzi have gathered information from conservation experts that shapes the way they will move and gesture with their own living bodies in the animals' world, and so their 'physical bearing in the world of the animal and how the animal reacts to their actions serves as a syntax for the pidgin language between species' (Broglio, 2008, p. 117). In the recording of the event, the scrawls and bites on the paper bear witness to and constitute the pidgin languages that arise from the animal–artist alliance in those contact zones. As Broglio explains:

> Art brings something back from this limit and horizon of the unknowable; it bears witness to encounters without falling into a language that assimilates or trivializes the world of the animal.

Given the immediacy and multimodality of these works, it's clear that the meaning of *Shark Bite* is not to be found in words and narratives imposed on the body of the animal. Rather, meaning emerges in the event, in the performance, in the experiential action between the participating human and non-human animals, when their whole being is not to be found in words, but rather in the living flesh of the animal—its gestures, its liveliness, fullness, and freedom to move in its world. In this sense, Olly and Suzi's work resists the closing down of meaning, the reduction to fixed, generic notions expressed in words and attached to sharks. One of Olly and Suzi's images that capture this experience of lively freedom is titled *Chasing Tail,* showing the tail of what appears to be a whale shark disappearing off to the left of the photograph with Olly and Suzi in diving gear following behind, peering intently in the direction of the shark and drawing together on a board held by Olly. The title appears to be an appropriation of the colloquial phrase used to indicate a sexual pursuit: chasing tail, a man chasing a woman, referred to by her body part, a tail. In this art work, the original concept of a heterosexual hunt is ironically repositioned as a collaborative human desire to appreciate and record the lively beauty of the shark as it swims away, free, and unfettered in its own environment. Human control over the animal is relinquished. In this case, the words and image work together to confuse and overturn heterosexist normativities, replacing them with a larger sense of shared wonder, joy, and engagement with the natural world of sharks in the ocean.

The purpose of Olly and Suzi's texts and performances is distinctive, as evidenced in comparison with Hirst's *Shark*. Hirst uses the bodies of dead animals, killed on his behalf and displayed in a glass box, to address questions of *human* mortality and to create a saleable commodity. In contrast, Olly and Suzi place their own bodies inside the cage which is in turn positioned within the animal's world, with the purpose of communicating as directly as possible not only the beauty of these sharks but also to communicate the extent to which their lives and habitats are under threat. This difference in textual purposes in turn shapes the artists' practices. Whereas Hirst distances himself from the living flesh of the shark, preferring to order one over the phone, for Olly and Suzi physical proximity to and interaction with sharks is integral to achieving their purpose: this is a process of 'witnessing . . . not knowing and consuming'; their works 'leave the mystery of the animal and its world intact while calling attention to its existence' (Broglio, 2011, p. 100).

The presence of Suzi Winstanley as a woman involved in producing this art work is significant in the process of resisting the overt machismo associated with shark hunting and Hirst's animal-based art, particularly his pickled *Shark*. Olly and Suzi's work with sharks and other animals is not overtly gendered, nor feminist. Instead, it demonstrates a collaborative, performative art practice in which both artists, and their animal participants, take part as equal partners. In this process, the will to dominate and control is surrendered. Neither Olly nor Suzi appears as an individual hero—let alone a heroic masculine hunter—and yet both experience the embodied work required to engage with animals in their wild habitats in order to bring back a message of urgent environmental importance. Their work is intimate and interactional, and as such stands as a rebuke to the violence and killing that lies at the heart of Hirst's animal installations.

One of my few concerns with Olly and Suzi's *Shark Bite* is that it risks reinforcing popular conceptions of the shark as an implacable and violent Other, although this is clearly not their intention. Indeed, Suzi asserts that their work with sharks is intended to 'show people that they're not just big scary animals' (cited in Baker, 2013, p. 32) and has expressed frustration that *Shark Bite* has 'continued to dominate public perception of their work' (p. 36). There is no guarantee, then, that their artworks, particularly as encapsulated in this compelling image, will support their desire to celebrate the beauty of sharks and contribute to preserving their significant place in a complex interconnected web of life. Public preconceptions of shark horror often appear to be resistant to change. In any case, Olly and Suzi's compromised efforts to address or challenge this preconception indicate yet again the difficulty that sharks present for any human attempts at reconciling and reconceptualising the relationship between human and non-human animals.

Sharks and Rays in Indigenous Australian Art

Another very different relationship between human and non-human animals, including sharks, is evident in the rich and varied art of Aboriginal and Torres Strait Islander Australians. These artistic expressions are inherently connected to a spiritual domain that links the present with the past and connects people with natural and supernatural beings. Spiritual life for Aboriginal and Torres Strait Islanders is realised in The Dreaming (a European term used to describe Aboriginal belief systems) which relates to the activities of supernatural beings and creator ancestors who, in human and non-human form, gave shape to the natural world—flora, fauna, humans, landforms, and celestial bodies—and provided an 'ideological framework by which human society retains a harmonious equilibrium with the universe' (Caruana, 2012, p. 10). Ancestral powers present in the land, waterways, flora, fauna, and individuals are activated, affirmed, and nourished through art and ceremony, such as dances, songs, and totemic associations.

As an expression of The Dreaming, Indigenous art in Australia comprises many distinct, long-established traditions or 'idioms' which are ancestrally inherited and contain a lexicon of designs, images, figures, and symbols that are potent carriers of meaning (Caruana, 2012). Interpretation of these designs and images is not through a simple one-to-one equivalence, a mistake sometimes made by Western art historians (McLean, 2016), but is rather more like poetry with all its intrinsic complexities, allusions, and ambiguities so that each image within a work may capture and communicate a variety of meanings (Caruana, 2012).

Two contemporary artists who have drawn on Indigenous heritage to express distinctive relationships between humans and sharks, or their close relatives the stingrays, are Torres Strait Islander Ken Thaiday Snr, and urban Aboriginal Lin Onus. Thaiday reinterprets traditional dance masks using modern materials to construct kinetic shark headdresses and hand-held 'dance machines' for use in public ceremonies, while Onus's paintings of stingray and dingo juxtapose images and symbols drawn from Aboriginal Australia with those from European settler culture to produce powerful political and spiritual statements.

Like many island communities, Torres Strait Islanders have a maritime culture that celebrates the deep relationship between people, the sea, and sea creatures. For Ken Thaiday's people on Erub (Darnley Island) the deep connection to water as place includes a relationship with the shark as an important totem: the 'boss of the saltwater, symbol of law and order' (Thaiday, cited in Bishop, 2013). In the 1980s, after his move to Cairns, Thaiday began constructing a visual repertoire of dance artefacts that use traditional symbolic language to connect Islander traditions and clan identity (Bishop, 2013). His best-known works are spectacular *Beizam* (Hammerhead Shark) headdresses which consist of a hammerhead shark (Thaiday's family totem) on top of a large shark's head, the whole made of bamboo, plywood, plastic, and wire, with white feathers that represent the sea foam around the body of the moving shark.[6] The headdresses are dynamic extensions of the human body, stretching upwards from the dancer's chest to high above the head and animated by the dancer pulling on strings to open and shut the shark's jaws and turn the shark's body back and forth.

Thaiday's inspiration is drawn not only from ancestral beliefs and traditions that pre-date colonisation but also from his Christian faith. Ironically, under British colonisation Christian missionaries and evangelists typically attempted to suppress traditional practices and promote Western customs. Yet in contemporary performances, it seems that Islander imagery, language, dances, songs, and stories have been seamlessly integrated with Christian ideas and inspiration (Lawrence & Lawrence, 2004).

Thaiday's sharks signal and celebrate a distinctive relationship between humans and these ocean animals, a relationship different to that represented in Western art traditions. The shark headdresses, animated in dances and songs, replenish these relationships and articulate an Aboriginal belief system in which the land, waterways, animals, and people are interdependent. In Thaiday's words 'When I'm dancing and wearing the Dari (headdress), I become the shark' (quoted in Eccles, 2017). This blurring of boundaries and subjectivities, so unfamiliar in Western discourse, is evident in Rothwell's (2013) description of the dance as a dynamic semiotic system where meaning emerges from the interplay of words, music, percussion, gesture, and movement of human and animal bodies:

> The headdress movements, the sounds of the dance, the singing, the musical rhythms and the beat of the rattles that the dancers bear all build into an image of ancestral power; the shark seems to live, and swim, and hunt, the red blood painted on its jaws becomes real. This is the art, born from years of close observation while fishing in the waters of the strait.
>
> (Rothwell, 2013)

A similar disruption of human–animal boundaries is articulated in the artwork of Lin Onus (1948–1996). An urban Aboriginal artist and activist of

Yorta Yorta and Scottish heritage, Onus developed a 'distinctive visual language', an 'accessible dialogue punctuated with wit and humour . . . that relies on inclusion rather than alienation for its impact' (Foley, 2000, p. 8). In his efforts to address social justice issues in a non-confrontational style, he saw his role as building a bridge between different societies and traditions with transcultural work that expressed a powerful politics and appealed to the contemporary mood for reconciliation. In the words of Margo Neale (2000a), Onus was 'a cultural terrorist of gentle irreverence' whose artistic works combine the mundane with the sacred 'whilst making potent political comment with humour'.

In the early 1990s, Onus produced a series of paintings under the broad title 'Ongoing adventures of X and Ray', based on the adventures of a dingo and a stingray, a close cartilaginous relative of the shark. In this series of satirical narrative works, Onus adopted the dingo (X) as a persona alongside the stingray (Ray), a metaphoric identity for his artist collaborator, Michael Eather. Onus identified with the figure of the dingo as a survivor of colonial misrepresentation, mistreatment, and dispossession, a wild dog hunted for its scalp and fenced off from its native feeding grounds. He politicised the animal by painting its coat with the red, black, and yellow bands of the Aboriginal flag, worn in the style of a football jumper. He inscribed his stingray friend with Indigenous *rarrk* markings—designs that signify clan affiliation—to indicate Eather's association with Arnhem Land and Aboriginal subjectivity (Ashcroft, 2013).

One of the best-known paintings from the series is the seminal work *Michael and I are just slipping down to the pub for a minute* (1992) in which Ray, the stingray, becomes a kind of surfboard for X, the dingo, as they ride perhaps the most famous wave in art history, an image appropriated from the 18th-century *Great Wave* woodcut by the Japanese artist Hokusai.[7]

As with the work of Ken Thaiday, most analyses of Onus's painting have focussed on its significance in terms of its engagement with transcultural identity in Australia, expressed through a powerful, translingual visual language that brings together refigured Indigenous idioms and Western realist ways of painting. In practices that are typical of his work, this painting mixes 'language and symbols and colours and messages, borrowing methods from Arnhem Land design, using graphic symbols and deft illustration' (Eather, 2000, p. 56). These various meaning-making sources are brought together in ways that break free from white Australia's expectations of traditional Aboriginal art, expectations that had been shaped by the prejudicial colonial science of anthropology. This practice of integrating indigenous spirituality, idiom, and narrative with Western representational systems produces an eclectic art that is both inventive and humorous. This is a painting that reaches across cultures and histories and anticipates the convergences of globalisation while, on a more personal level, encapsulating Onus's kinship networks, life, and art (Neale, 2000b).

The painting also speaks to us about different ways of imagining human–animal entanglements in material and discursive worlds, offering additional meanings that speak to possible new futures. From my own perspective, further meanings emerge from a close reading of the wave and the figure of the stingray.

Hokusai's iconic woodblock print of *The Great Wave* was produced near the end of Japan's two centuries of seclusion from the world and depicts a towering wave much larger than Mount Fuji and about to engulf three tiny fishing boats. The image of a rogue wave sweeping away everything in its path seems prescient in its foreshadowing of the momentous changes brought about by the arrival in 1853 of U.S. naval forces demanding that Japan end its long period of isolation and open its ports to trade with the West. The subsequent commercial arrangements negotiated between the two nations were highly disadvantageous to the Japanese and signalled a major shift in the balance of power between the West and Japan. At the same time, on the Australian continent, Indigenous owners of the land were suffering the full onslaught of British invasion. Onus has taken an image produced in this historical time and turned it upside down: instead of a fearful monstrous wave about to swamp the tiny human figures in Hokusai's original print, we have a wave that offers an opportunity for collaboration, celebration, and conciliation, represented in the figures of dingo and the stingray as they ride together on the crest of the wave with obvious playfulness and pleasure. The wave, the animals, and the artists combine in a collective force, reclaiming and revisioning history.

Originating in Indigenous spiritual ancestry, the stingray and the dingo are figures of hybrid vigour, of shape-shifting therianthropy rather than simple anthropomorphism. Instead of the animal bodies providing the grounds for the projection of human characteristics, the human artists—Onus and Eather—have *become* the dingo and stingray. In this practice the traditional boundaries that maintain the distinctions between poisonous stingray and human, and between dangerous dingo and human, are breached and blurred: human and non-human are mutually animating agents. This animal–human blurring then opens the way for other binaries—between Indigenous and non-Indigenous, tradition, and modernity, nature and culture, high art and popular culture—to be disrupted. If we accept Neale's (2000b, p. 20) reading of Ray as a *female* stingray, then gender binaries are also collapsed in this image of shape-shifting collaboration. Energised in a mood of hybrid vigour and subversion, the figures in the painting are extraordinarily hopeful. The stingray and the dingo, atop the wave, are forward-facing, in advancing motion, full of kinetic energy; their gaze is directed beyond the frame of the picture, as they surf together into the future.

Looking Back, Looking Forward

The multimodal languages of art offer us a way of understanding human relationships with other animals and also a means of revisioning and reconstructing that relationship. As Aloi (2011, p. xx) points out, art offers us a means of 'capturing the complexities of nature' in a way that science, despite its 'evidential validity', does not. Yet artistic representation of the world is, like science and the verbal arts, limited, partial, and shaped by the viewpoint of human proclivities, perspectives, and desires. Representations of our relationships with sharks and their stingray kin have too often been constructed through discourses that serve to reflect back to humans certain gendered and patriarchal visions of society, and pit heroic masculinity against wild nature. After all, 'representation of the world, like the world itself, is the work of men; they describe it from their own point of view, which they confuse with absolute truth' (de Beauvoir, 1972, p. 61).

Yet art can also offer representations and invitations to a different relationship between humans and the more-than-human world. This might be a means of entanglement that is both discursive and material, that escapes the monomodal understanding of the shark (and other creatures) as deserving of slaughter, and instead sets her free.

Notes

1. *Perseus and Andromeda*, by Titian (1554–1556). Available at: https://wallace live.wallacecollection.org/eMP/eMuseumPlus?service=ExternalInterface&mod ule=collection&objectId=64901&viewType=detailView
2. *Watson and the shark*, by John Singleton Copley (1782). Available at: www.dia. org/art/collection/object/watson-and-the-shark-41300
3. *Rape of the daughters of Leucippus*, by Peter Paul Rubens (1615–1618). Available at: www.wikiart.org/en/peter-paul-rubens/rape-of-the-daughters-of-leucippus-1618
4. *The physical impossibility of death in the mind of someone living*, by Damien Hirst (1991). Available at http://damienhirst.com/the-physical-impossibility-of
5. *Shark Bite*, by Olly and Suzi (photograph by Greg Williams) (1997). Available at: www.ollysuzi.com/photographs/shark-bite/
6. *Beizam (shark) dance mask*, by Ken Thaiday (1997). Available at: www.artgallery. nsw.gov.au/collection/works/4.1997/
7. *Michael and I are just slipping down to the pub for a minute*, by Lin Onus (1992). Available at: www.moadoph.gov.au/blog/artists-and-activists-the-ongoing-adventures-of-x-and-ray/

4   Surfing With Sharks

According to postcolonial scholar Helen Tiffin (2010), Australians have since European settlement, 'cheerfully played "the last frontier" to the United States' loss of it'. Here in Australia, she continues, 'men are men and sharks are sharks and Australians still have the courage and know-how to take on the creatures of the wild' (p. 67). The shark has a major role to play, then, in the construction of a particular type of Australian hegemonic masculinity: pugnacious, outdoorsy, and nonchalant in the face of danger. As Tiffin notes, some years ago performer Paul Hogan as *Crocodile Dundee* and television personality Steve Irwin as *The Crocodile Hunter* were projecting images of knockabout bravado that Australia seems proud to present for audiences in the USA and Britain. At the time, as a consequence of its role in this drama, the crocodile threatened to 'dislodge the shark from its position as Australia's greatest symbolic terror' (p. 73).

But in recent years the shark has made a spectacular comeback. In 2015 the International Shark Attack File (ISAF) reported 98 unprovoked shark bite incidents, the most ever recorded in a single year. More than half of these occurred in the USA, with particularly high counts in Florida and the Carolinas, and a further quarter occurred in Australia. Around the world, almost all these incidents—around 95% of cases including the rare fatalities—involved men: men surfing, men bodyboarding, men skindiving, men spearfishing. And yet human–shark encounters, and the network of activities that surround them, are rarely discussed as a gendered event.

Although there was much discussion about the reason for the increase in shark incidents in recent years, a rational assessment suggested that the number of human–shark interactions correlated directly with the increasing amount of time that people spend in aquatic recreation activities (West, 2011). It's perhaps unsurprising, then, that surfers are now the group most likely to have close encounters with sharks. The entanglement of surfers and sharks is the topic of this chapter, and this entanglement provides a focus for a broader consideration of the political and cultural meaning of sharks, surfing, the beach, and gender in Australia.

Sharks in News Media

Australian writer and surfer, Tim Winton (2013), wryly observes that the reason God made sharks was to sell newspapers, and every year our news media lavishes attention on any incidents of human–shark interaction. In 2009, the media announced we were experiencing Australia's 'summer of shark terror' (Callinan, 2009), after seven shark attacks were recorded within the space of a month, including one fatality. Over an even longer period in 2014–2016 the media in Australia seemed to be saturated with panic-style stories about sharks, complete with lurid pictures and alarmist headlines. In the summer of 2017, a headline in the *Sydney Morning Herald* (SMH, Jan 7–8 2017) simply read 'Shark!', followed by a leader paragraph asking: 'Have a spate of bites and sightings up and down the NSW coast raised the odds that an attack awaits beachgoers this summer?' This genre of headline and story is never far from public view in Australia, and as I write the media gaze is focussed on two incidents of sharks biting swimmers in the same waters of the Great Barrier Reef off the coast of Queensland.

In this flurry of media attention, issues of gender are rarely (if ever) mentioned, explored, or explained. It is only in academic studies, from fields as diverse as cultural studies, history, sociology, and geography that explicit recognition has been given to the gendered and sexualised construction of surfing culture. In these studies, surfing has often been figured as primarily a masculine, white, heterosexual culture, engaged in the heroic quest: the search, challenge, and competition for the perfect wave. In line with this 'hard core image', one of the most popular surfboard designs emerging in previous decades and still popular today was the so-called 'thruster', a three-finned short board which privileges aggression over aesthetics and enjoyment, and 'masculinises the surfing experience even through its name' (Stedman, 1997, p. 82). In language that signals man-against-nature, waves are 'killed' through 'deadly' manoeuvres that 'rip', 'slash', and 'cut', and the hyper-masculine style of performance does little to 'destabilise the power of regulatory gender fictions between the land-as-civilised and the ocean-as-wild' (Waitt, 2008, p. 76). Research suggests that women are increasingly participating in surfing, with somewhat surprising estimates that around one-third of the surfers in the USA and Australia are female (Booth, 2001; Bush, 2016; Roy Morgan Research, 2015). Yet despite the increasing number of female surfers in recent years, Roy and Caudwell (2014) suggest that women have been recruited into a discourse of the 'hetero-sexy' female surfer as a 'valuable icon' of the surf industry, while 'discourses of exclusion which serve to maintain masculine heterosexuality remain valued within surfing culture' (p. 235).

The predominance of male surfers is also closely aligned with the predominance of men in shark attack statistics. In the peak year of 2015 in Australia, for example, the Global Shark Attack File (GSAF) recorded 23 unprovoked incidents involving male interactions with sharks, including two fatalities. Only one incident involved a female, a seven-year-old girl who was swimming with her family in shallow waters off Queensland coast. From a total of 180 unprovoked human–shark incidents recorded in Australia over the last ten years (2007–2016), 101 (56%) involved surfers, but only five of those surfers were female. Men were involved in the remaining 95% of incidents involving surfers and sharks (GSAF). Given the purported increase in the number of women involved in surfing over recent years, the incidence of women and girls involved in reported human–shark interactions is remarkably small.

Men also feature heavily in media stories where surfers meet sharks, but in such accounts gender, as such, never gets an explicit mention. The male experience is treated as a universal truth. Nevertheless, gender emerges obliquely in the sorts of discourses that permeate these stories and in the subsequent audience commentary they elicit. Media reports of human–shark encounters, because they almost always involve men, provide great scope for the construction of Australian masculinity.

Surfing With the Great White Shark

Arguably the most spectacular human–shark incident involving an Australian in recent years didn't occur in Australia; it unfolded in Jeffrey's Bay (J-Bay), South Africa, during the World Surfing League (WSL) men's 2015 tour series. The live broadcast of the event captured the moment when world champion Australian surfer Mick Fanning, competing in the Open finals, was tumbled from his surfboard in a tussle with a great white shark (World Surf League, 2015).[1] The spoken utterances that accompany the video broadcast convey the immediacy, shock, and unexpected drama of the event, and the alarm induced by the encounter. The video broadcast opens with a view of Fanning's head and torso as he sits on his surf board waiting for a wave, and a large black shark fin appears beside him:

BROADCASTER A: . . . the last season, as you look at Fanning on the rankings—oh—can see a little splash—
[shark fin, splashing, Fanning tumbled from board, then a rising wave obscures all sight of Fanning and the shark for several seconds]
BROADCASTER B: Oh—holy shit,'scuse me

[VOICE FROM BEACH LOUDSPEAKERS]: [unintelligible] get Fanning immediately! now! get Fanning immediately! get out there immediately! get there now!

BROADCASTER A: looks like Fanning . . .

[VOICE FROM BEACH LOUDSPEAKERS]: [unintelligible]

BROADCASTER A: Fanning needing some assistance, he's swimming into the beach [siren sounds] as we sound the horn to stop the final. Fanning still swimming on his own right, to the assistance of the jet skis, he'll hop on the sled and re-set, so climbing up, with his own ability, as he keeps his head down, Fanning with a thumbs up, he is ok, rushing to the water safety, his leash chewed off as he shakes this one off, as we're gonna clear the line up now to let Fanning catch his breath

[VOICE FROM BEACH LOUDSPEAKERS]: All surfers get out of the water immediately!

BROADCASTER A: but a big sigh of relief seeing Fanning in one piece, as we saw the fin out the back, wow . . .

Fanning had escaped shaken but unharmed, and was whisked away by a jet ski sent to his rescue. The competition was cancelled and prize money split amongst the finalists. In the following days a wave of media reports appeared, describing and commenting on the encounter from various perspectives and representing the surfer and the shark in a variety of ways.

The mainstream Australian news media picked up the event with alacrity. The first set of reports, published the day after the event, foregrounded the more alarmist tone of fear, and the underlying discourse of a pugnacious frontier masculinity ascribed to Fanning. In the *Daily Telegraph* (Walker, 2015) and *The Sydney Morning Herald* (Knox, 2015) the event was reported in ways that encapsulated and reproduced the fear of death that sharks have come to represent, and simultaneously reproduced the male surfer hero discourses.

The *Daily Telegraph* headline, 'Fanning fights off killer shark in shock surf final', and the *Sydney Morning Herald* headline, 'Mick Fanning shark attack one of the most surreal near-death experiences seen on live TV', clearly indicate the discursive frames used to represent the encounter. The reports also show the human–animal–machine assemblage in action: Fanning the surfer, the shark as uncanny symbol of horror and death, and the struggle captured by the technology of television and watched online over the coming days and weeks by millions of spectators. Throughout these texts, the event is represented in terms of a particular discourse that could be described as 'Man-eating shark defeated by Aussie hero'. The *Daily Telegraph* report described a 'monster shark' with 'razor-sharp teeth' that 'tore through the 34-year-old's leg rope and tried to drag the three-time world champion off his board'; but Fanning fought like a real man, he 'punched' the shark and escaped 'shaken' but unharmed (Walker, 2015). In the *Sydney Morning Herald*, the shark attack was presented as 'something horrible and macabre . . . that strikes deep notes in our fear of nature', 'a sickening and frightening sight', and Fanning was idolised as 'a hero to children and adults' whose brush 'with mortality' illustrates 'the risks surfers take' in the ocean (Knox, 2015). In these reports, Mick Fanning emerges as the very essence of a great white male hero conquering a raw and brutal natural world. By the end of the year, along the same lines, Fanning's shark triumph was counted on several lists of Australia's greatest sporting achievements of 2015.

Media stories from outside Australia also reported the Fanning incident but were more tempered and tended to situate the event within a broader set of discourses about typical shark behaviour, the rarity of attacks, and shark conservation. These were presented as 'expert' discourses from the supposedly more neutral worlds of science and statistics. A report from South Africa posted in the UK *Telegraph* ran the headline 'Small Great White shark did not intend to kill surfer Mick Fanning, say experts' (Laing, 2015). Laing emphasised that the incident involved 'a fairly young, small Great White' that was 'investigating' rather than 'intending to attack the surfer'. The report quoted a South African shark expert and tourism promoter who urged that 'people should not be put off from venturing into South African waters'. An environment reporter for *The Guardian* in the USA (Milman, 2015) similarly drew on shark science research with the headline 'Sharks don't like to eat people: Attack statistics contradict untested theories'. Milman presented expert evidence to debunk popular theories about a 'dangerous escalation in shark numbers', arguing that the increased incidence of shark encounters in 2015 was a consequence of an increasing human population and a rise in the popularity of water-based activities. He reiterated the logic-based truth that 'the chances of being attacked are extremely small' and contrasted this with reports that 100 million sharks are killed each year, many for shark fin soup.

A science-based perspective was also circulated in articles that appeared in an online, open access forum for academic commentary, *The Conversation*, where specialists in shark research used the incident as a platform to plead for a more rational response to the presence of sharks in the ocean. While these articles acknowledged the fear induced by Fanning's experience, they moved quickly to arguments based on scientific reasoning. Gibbs (2015), for example, briefly acknowledged the concerns raised by the Fanning incident, but then pointed out that the risk of harm from any shark interaction is 'incredibly low'. Gibbs critiqued the government's shark culling policies, and cited Neff and Hueter's (2013) proposal to change the emotive, fear-inducing, and misleading language around shark 'attacks' in favour of the graded set of descriptors that more precisely indicate the type of human–shark interaction that has occurred. Gibbs's closing observation that 'Fanning's close shave reminds us we share the ocean', is a plea for coexistence and shark rights that is increasingly evident in contemporary social media commentary. Similarly, Burgess (2015) acknowledges that the Fanning incident has provoked fears that are 'understandable' and 'sensible', but then moves to his main argument that sharks, as apex predators, are indispensable to healthy marine ecosystems. Burgess cites research studies bearing the 'good news' that shark numbers are increasing, and emphasises that humans will need to 'relearn how to live alongside them'.

On social media platforms, an even broader range of discourses was emerging. Audience comments appearing below the online YouTube video of the Fanning event demonstrate competing but interrelated themes that overlap, extend, and overturn the discourses evident in traditional media. The first typifies the traditional fear response in relation to shark-as-monster, summarised by this apt phrase: 'that was some scary shit'. The second exemplifies the voice of eco-reason, also seen in traditional media, playing down the fear factor and introducing a stable scientistic discourse: 'This was a tame encounter with an apex predator of the ocean'. The third group of comments illustrates the sort of gallows humour typical of social media while also indexing the hero masculinity associated with Australian surfing:

> lucky for the shark got away with just a punch on the back. he probably didn't realised the surfer was Australian.
> Surfer? This is 2 times world champion Mick Fanning
> How can that man float with balls that big?

But in some of these humorous responses, something more anarchic is evident. In these examples, the shark regains some agency in the incident, occupying the subject position and in some cases providing the primary point of view:

> The shark was obviously just a fan. . . . He probably wanted an autograph, or a selfie with the surfer or something.
> The way the shark came out was like 'Peek-a-boo'!
> If the shark had a YouTube channel, the video is probably called: 'scaring people! PRANK GONE WRONG!!' In the description will be like: I was trying to scare the dude, so that I could get some good reactions. But out of nowhere! The guy jumped on my back and punched me! And so I tried to fend myself by slapping him with my fins.

But the idea of Fanning the great white hero who punches the great white shark seemed to have more popular appeal than any message of shark conservation or shark agency, so much so that within a week of the incident, the *Daily Telegraph* proposed that 'Punched a shark' be adopted as a 'new phrase for the sporting lexicon', and recommended that the term 'should now be used to describe those acts of physical and mental courage and heroism on (and near) the sporting field in the face of overwhelming odds' (Hinds, 2015). Punching the shark also quickly became the topic of multiple internet memes which appeared within a day of the J-Bay shark encounter. These images delight in the same humour as the comments that followed the WSL broadcast video and endlessly circulate the discourse of pugnacious heroism, picturing Fanning variously punching, riding, and holding the shark aloft like a trophy. The shark is shown variously dejected and defeated, or full of admiration for the human champion. One of my personal favourites is the *Jaws* poster parody, a cleverly intertextual image that reverses the positioning of shark and victim in the original. In the parody version, Fanning's glowering image is below the water line in the predator position, his brow lowered menacingly and with eyes gazing upwards in the direction of the shark. The shark is a smaller figure swimming at the water surface, in the position of the original naked female victim. In place of the large-print JAWS at the top of the poster, we have MICK in bold red; and in place of the widely quoted phrase from the movie, 'You're gonna need a bigger boat', we have 'You're gonna need a bigger shark'. This is an upside-down world, and yet one that is very familiar in its gendered and anthropocentric hierarchies: Mick, surfing hero, undefeated, the white man in mastery over wild nature.

But this joyous celebration of the Aussie male wasn't the only theme that emerged in those years of peak human–shark interactions. While the Fanning memes captured the humour of the moment, it was more frequently the fear and alarm associated with shark attacks that held sway in the mainstream media. From the beginning of 2014 through to the end of 2016, the Global Shark Attack File recorded 67 unprovoked human–shark encounters in Australia, only seven of which involved women or girls. Most of these events provoked media panic, particularly when the human involved suffered serious injuries. In these accounts—as in the Fanning incident—a common trope was the male hero exercising a powerful agency in a vicious battle against the marauding shark. One widely reported attack was on a male surfer and ex-champion boxer who 'described how he fought the shark in a life-and-death duel' (Banks, 2015). In the *Daily Telegraph*, Banks reported the surfer's account with expletives deleted:

It was personal. He was saying to me 'don't even bother thinking you're going to get out of this one mate, you're f . . . ed, I've got you no worries', Mr Ison said. 'But I said to the shark, "f . . . you, I'll fight dirty too". . . .'His jaws were just ripping and tearing and I'm there just looking at it, I thought 'I better do something' so I went bang, bang, bang, bang and punched him four times and he let go.

Similar reports kept the media busy with the now-familiar storyline informing readers of men's fighting prowess. Under the headline 'Ryan goes to war against Jaws', one such account describes how 'A shark attack victim was forced to strike and wrestle off the savage predator, mauling him before escaping to the safety of the beach in a bloodied and injured state' (Townsend, 2014). Where surfing men became fighting heroes, sharks became the enemy to be feared, and the media demonised the enemy with dramatic accounts and sensational language. Much of this language has become entrenched in our cultural imaginary and echoes Spielberg's 1975 movie *Jaws*, a form of public pedagogy which persists as a 'touchstone for media reporting' (Francis, 2011, p. 56) and much of the language used by the media.

By 2015, the *Australian* newspaper was reporting that 'protected killer sharks', 'monsters on our shores', were now aggressively 'lured towards humans' (Ross, 2015). The *Sydney Morning Herald* advised us to 'Be alert, be afraid' in the face of 'the truth about shark attacks' (Robson, 2015). And the *Daily Telegraph* named NSW 'the shark capital of the world, with 12 unprovoked attacks so far this year—including one death and six serious maulings—mostly on the un-netted north coast' (Godfrey, 2015). Clichéd intertextual phrases such as 'Jaws of death' (Keene, 2015) became commonplace, along with the predictable lexicon of silent 'killer sharks', 'monsters' and 'predators', threatening, prowling, stalking, menacing, and attacking humans. As anthropologist Adrian Peace (2015) points out, these words serve to project onto sharks, especially great whites, the criminal or immoral intent and behaviour of humans, demonising them in the same way that humans marked by difference are demonised. Killer sharks are also blamed for violating spatial boundaries: they intrude into territory— beaches, harbours, shallow waters—where humans have decided they don't rightly belong, in the same way that certain categories of humans are designated as unwelcome intruders when entering spaces that are zoned for sole use by more privileged groups.

A range of conflicting reasons was offered to explain the high incidence of human–shark encounters in the years 2014 to 2016. Perhaps the spike in attacks was due to the (over)protection of great whites, or the lack of shark nets. Perhaps there was an unusual abundance of bait fish, or a depletion of sharks' natural food sources. Perhaps it was warming of ocean waters. No one had a definitive answer, and uncertainty fuelled the media panic.

As one 'ocean aficionado' observed in *The Saturday Paper*, 'We are in the dark' (Chenery, 2015). From a feminist perspective, I might observe that 'in the dark' may be a fearful place for surfers who venture into the ocean, but 'the dark' is also a place of fearfulness for so many women and girls who are conditioned to restrict their movements and ways of being even on land.

The language used in conventional media reports of shark-related incidents involving women and girls is often quite different to that used in reports involving men. Reports about female victims are, to begin with, relatively rare, since most attacks involve male surfers and hunters diving for fish or abalone. In 2014, three of the 20 unprovoked human–shark interactions recorded in Australia by the GSAF did involve women. One of the women, the subject of a report in the *Daily Telegraph* and the *Gold Coast Bulletin*, is identified as 'a barmaid' who 'after having a few drinks' on a Saturday night 'fell into' river water 'at about 9:30pm' (Ardern & Wurth, 2014). In this and other reports of the incident, there's a familiar message of victim blaming directed at a reckless foolish woman: not only was she drinking, but she 'entered the water at night when [shark] activity increases'. Although this species of shark 'tends to avoid humans', in this case it 'would have been drawn to' the victim 'because she was splashing and treading water'. The woman is even quoted as accepting the blame for intruding on a shark that she refers to, through pronoun use, as male: 'It was not the shark's fault . . . it was my fault. I am sure I interrupted him and gave him a fright'.

Only one of the 11 shark encounters with Australian surfers in 2014 involved a female, a young teenage woman surfing on the NSW central coast (GSAF). Unlike the dramatic reporting style reserved for attacks on male surfers, the reports of this incident were light-hearted. In click-bait style, the *Daily Telegraph* headlined with 'I screamed like hell', but then noted that the attack involved not the usually voracious great white or tiger shark, but 'a normally docile wobbegong'. Despite suffering deep gashes on her leg which required surgery, the teenager, described as a 'smiling grommet' (young surfer), 'started laughing' as she paddled to the shore, and was still laughing when she left the water (Noone, 2014).

Of the five shark-related fatalities recorded in Australia in 2014, just one involved a woman (GSAF). Reports of this incident, involving an older female swimmer on the NSW south coast, show a surprising lack of agency either on the part of the woman or the shark. There is no fighting or punching, there are no heroes, the woman simply disappears, and in most reports the shark is never seen. Both slip away silently, invisibly, into the ocean. In just one account, a man on the shore sees a shark 'tussle with an object in the water' (Robinson & Nadin, 2014). An object, a woman. A message of victim blaming is evident in these accounts, too. Robinson and Nadin (2014) observe an air 'complacency' about sharks in this location; other reports note that there had been 'warnings' about sharks in the area, so an attack was inevitable, a 'tragedy waiting to happen' (Page, Belot & Westacott, 2014). Moreover, the woman had turned back to swim 'alone, as she often did', away from her group, and was 'taken' and killed by the shark (Page, Belot & Westacott, 2014). She had made a 'fateful decision' to go her own way (Chambers & Lion, 2014), and so was swimming against an historical tide of warnings directed at controlling the movement of women and girls.

Media reports sometimes choose to carry advice on how to minimise the risk of attack by a shark in words that echo the discourses surrounding the sole female swimmer fatally attacked in 2014. Neil Keene's (2015) 'Jaws of death' story, reflecting on the Mick Fanning incident and pondering the apparent spike in shark attacks in Australia, exemplifies such advice and is replete with patterns of language that are eerily familiar to women. In order to be safe in the ocean, we're told to avoid venturing out in the dim light of dawn and dusk when sharks are likely to be on the prowl; avoid venturing into the sea alone; avoid remote areas, stay with a group; avoid murky waters where sharks may be lurking, unseen. Away from the ocean environment, these are common enough warnings directed at women and girls. Perhaps, for men they strike a more confronting and discordant note of unfamiliar fear.

Bite Club, Gender, and the Shift for Sharks

In the peak shark years, while the mainstream media continued to publish sensational reports of gruesome shark attacks on unsuspecting men, there was evidence of a gradual shift in public opinion about sharks and their place in the environment. Across Australia in 2013 and 2014 there were unprecedented pro-shark rallies attracting thousands across Australia, protesting against a shark 'cull' executed with baited drum lines and sponsored by the Western Australia government after seven fatal shark attacks in that state between 2010 and 2013. The protests brought surfers together with environmental and animal rights activists, celebrities, and scientists, at beaches from Perth in the west right across the nation to my local ocean beach on the east coast.

At the same time, on social media platforms there was increasing evidence of negative public comments directed at victims of shark attacks. This pattern was of particular concern for a group of surfers and shark attack survivors calling themselves the *Bite Club*, a name that references the millennial movie *Fight Club*. This movie had been a pugnacious response to the threats posed by second-wave feminism and a celebration of men's resurgent potency performed through violent and brutal bare-fisted fights. A media story on the Bite Club was illustrated with photographs of the men standing, facing the camera, displaying wounds, or running into the surf, and provided details of each shark attack (Dapin, 2016). The main question asked by the author was why these shark attack survivors had been subjected to hostility and victim-blaming on social media: 'Why are they treated as ocean intruders getting their just desserts?' (Dapin, 2016). When reading contemporary media accounts of their own experiences, the men recalled that the readers' comments section included offensive posts such as 'This idiot! Why does he deserve any attention?' 'He was surfing in the dark', 'He knew there was heaps of fish out there'. The founder of the Bite Club noted that in social media

> The posts will typically run: 'What was the surfer doing in the water? It's the shark's ocean anyway;' 'Oh, how surprising! A shark in the ocean;' 'This guy's a fool. He shouldn't be surfing. It's his own fault he got attacked'.

The posts were 'personally aggressive towards the shark attack survivor', and critical of victims 'for having the audacity to go into the ocean and get attacked' (Dapin, 2016).

Given the increasing emphasis on marine conservation and the rise of the No Shark Cull movement, the hostility directed at shark attack victims might be prompted by a broader change in the underlying public discourse about sharks: a drift towards greater respect for these animals and their integral role as apex predators in maintaining healthy oceans (see Hoskins, 2014; King, 2014). This shift in favour of shark conservation has been evident in the relative rarity of media calls for sharks to be targeted for killing, criticism of government-sponsored retaliation culling (Wolfe, 2018), and the more frequent publication of calm, ecology-focused articles interspersed with more typically sensationalist 'true-*Jaws*' media accounts of shark attacks (Francis, 2011, p. 52). Negative comments directed at shark bite victims might also be a reaction against the descriptions of male trauma and mutual support evident in the accounts of Bite Club members. Are stories of hurt and caring an affront to an invulnerable, heroic masculinity that characterises Australian nationalism? Or perhaps the negative responses are simply symptomatic of the licence taken by some users of social media to post vitriolic personal attacks, particularly where gender identity is an issue.

But here again, a gendered comparison is instructive. Whereas the relatively small number of men belonging to the Bite Club have experienced damaging online attacks, the vast majority of stalking, harassment, and victim-blaming online is directed at women and has been recognised as a practice of silencing and excluding women from the (digital) public sphere (Megarry, 2014). A similar gender imbalance is apparent in physical attacks:

where the rare cases of shark attacks *on men* receive an inordinate amount of media coverage, there is relative silence surrounding the wave of misogynistic intimidation and violence against women *by men* in cyberspace, on the streets, and in the home. Compared to the 159 recorded shark attacks on men in Australia over the last decade, the reported incidence of violence against women is remarkably high, with one in every four women having experienced physical or sexual violence by an intimate partner since the age of 15 (Cox, 2015).

While cases of extreme physical violence against women in Australia are considered by the media to be newsworthy events, in the reporting of these events male perpetrators are rendered largely invisible or are provided excuses to diminish their culpability (Sutherland et al., 2016). Media reports of male violence against women tend to focus on single events, as if they were isolated, random happenings, rather than part of a broad pattern of male domination and coercive control. Contrast this with the frequency of media reports that focus on clusters, spikes, and patterns of shark attacks over several months or years. Moreover, in terms of the type of events reported in the media, Sutherland et al. (2016, p. 31) find a general neglect of 'some of the most insidious forms of gender-based violence—emotional and psychological abuse . . . and other forms of intimidating and controlling behaviours'. Where cases are reported, varieties of victim-blaming are evident (Easteal, Holland & Judd, 2015). Together, these practices of silence and silencing have enabled a 'pattern of violence against women that's broad and deep and horrific and incessantly overlooked' (Solnit, 2014, p. 20), and have 'allowed predators to rampage through the decades, unchecked' (Solnit, 2017, p. 22).

It may be a commonplace that 'there are few fears for Australians as perennial as shark attack' (Hoskins, 2014). But is this pronounced fear an outcome of gendered apprehension? Is this fear of sharks so widely publicised because shark attacks are mostly experienced by men, whereas women's experiences and fears of verbal, emotional, sexual, and physical attacks perpetrated by men are so ubiquitous as to be natural and unremarkable?

Men, Women and the Right to Bodily Integrity and Freedom

So what are we to make of this complex of men, the media, and shark-related frenzy? One argument might be that men are doubly affronted by the threat posed by sharks. Records suggest that men are the most likely to be involved in shark encounters, and the potential horror of a shark encounter is heightened by the sort of media coverage that such incidents attract. At the same time, it seems plausible that for men there is an unspoken assumption that they have a right to pass unhindered wherever they choose to go.

Perhaps men are not conditioned to be wary of harassment (either benign of malignant) and intrusions (touching, interfering, groping). Women are conditioned to be wary and vigilant, to guard against such intrusions from an early age. As Deborah Cameron (2016, para. 18) observes, such forced intrusions 'are more than just irritants: they're part of the apparatus that's used to subordinate and control us'.

> Catcalling, casual touching, groping, unwanted personal comments or sexual overtures, being followed on the street, being verbally abused or threatened if you ignore a man's demand for your attention—these are everyday experiences for women in public places, and they all rest on the assumption that any man has an automatic right to treat any woman as an intimate: get close to her, touch her, make demands of her.
>
> (Cameron, 2016, para. 18)

The right of women to bodily integrity, and a lifelong experience of men's attempts to colonise and control the bodies of women: is there an analogy here with the shark's uninvited, unwanted attention directed to the bodies of men—men who are not used to this sort of bodily violation? Men may be understandably troubled, fearful, and aghast at having to be wary in the ocean, but it seems that almost all women have a lifelong wariness about violation in public and private domains.

Note

1. *Shark attacks Mick Fanning at the J-Bay open 2015*. Available at: www.youtube.com/watch?v=anhRxIQutZ8

5   Shark Science

In an essay on animal sociology four decades ago, Donna Haraway (1978) observed that 'We polish an animal mirror to look for ourselves' (p. 37). In particular, Haraway was interested at that time in the ways in which misleading scientific interpretations of sex and reproduction in primates had been used to legitimate beliefs in the natural necessity of normative gendered behaviours and hierarchies in human society. Over succeeding decades, these ideas have been taken up in a wide range of scholarship investigating the way that studies in animal science, with their purported production of objective universal truths, have reflected myths and theories about human behaviour, particularly in regard to sexuality and sex roles.

The promulgation of these conservative gender myths in popular wildlife films and nature television programmes has also been a focus of feminist critique (for example, Birke, 2002; Coward, 1984; Crowther, 1995, 1999; Crowther & Leith, 1995; Chris, 2006). In these critiques of the wildlife genre, textual analysis has demonstrated the prevalence of anthropomorphism and its effects in shaping the perceptions of scientific researchers and their interpretation of animal behaviours. As Crowther (1999) argues, 'conventional (heterosexual) male attitudes to women, and male interests and perceptions, are regularly reflected in the way animals' behaviour is interpreted and represented' in wildlife films (p. 46). When these partial assumptions about gender and sexuality are projected onto nature in terms of gender stereotypes, we're frequently presented with accounts of 'macho males and coy females' (Birke, 2002, p. 430) which can then be conveniently reflected back to human populations as biological explanations for supposedly natural human sexual behaviours.

In this chapter, I explore the way conservative discourses of gender and sexuality are still evident in contemporary accounts of animal science, both in authoritative academic journals and in popular science websites and videos. I consider several stories that illustrate just some of the ways in which scientific investigations into and publications about sharks are entangled with the gendered stories that humans tell about themselves, their origins, their behaviours, and their purported position at the top of an evolutionary tree.

The Mother Fish and the Penis

In 2008 Australian scientists reported, in the journal *Nature*, a remarkable discovery: fossil remains of the world's oldest mother, a shark-like placoderm ancestor of the sharks we know today, holding 'a small internal individual', an embryo, attached by an umbilical cord within the mother's body (Long et al., 2008, p. 650). The placoderm fossil represents the oldest example of any creature giving birth to live young—viviparity—as opposed to laying eggs for external fertilisation like their fish ancestors did, thus presenting the earliest evidence of an advanced form of reproduction involving copulation and internal fertilisation most often associated with mammals. This ancient mother 'extends the record of vertebrate viviparity back by some 200 million years' (Long et al., 2008, p. 650): previously, the earliest records of viviparity were from marine reptiles in the Jurassic period—the age of the dinosaurs—dating back to around 180 million years ago (Dennis, 2008).

The 380-million-year-old fossil mother was found in the Gogo formation, a fossil site in Australia's Kimberley region renowned for its superb three-dimensional specimens. The newly discovered species was named *Materpiscis* [mother fish] *attenboroughi*, after Sir David Attenborough, who drew world attention to the Gogo area when he visited the site for his *Life on Earth* television series in 1979. Despite this geographic connection, there is something ironic (though perhaps not surprising) about the world's oldest pregnant mother being called into language with the name of a human male.

In the wake of the *Materpiscis* finding, some previously unearthed placoderm specimens, kept in storage around the world, were subject to a revised interpretive reading, with the result that more examples of previously undetected embryos were found. This sense of *reading* the stones to decipher or translate meaning is evidenced in the palaeontologist's description of returning to another placoderm fossil that he had found some 20 years earlier:

> Scrutinizing it under higher microscope magnification and using the first discovery of the embryo as *our Rosetta Stone*, I could see that features that I had originally interpreted as dislodged scales were in fact tiny bones belonging to embryos. We had found another ancient mother, one that had died at the prime of life with triplets inside her.
>
> (Long, 2011, p. 38)

Fitting the placoderm mothers into an evolutionary narrative, finding her relatives and descendants, was a related task. Although placoderms, the world's first megapredators, are thought to be close ancestral relatives of sharks and rays (cartilaginous fishes collectively known as elasmobranchs), the exact relationship between the two is a subject of ongoing debate (Ahlberg, 2009). Placoderms are now extinct, but those ancient sharks and rays are still with us in the form of highly evolved living descendants with large brains and complex social and sexual behaviour (Pratt & Carrier, 2001). Like their placoderm ancestors, modern female sharks and rays have a particular reproductive strategy: the females have few progeny and most rear them internally before releasing them as well-developed juveniles. These offspring are larger and hardier than those resulting from the riskier process of mass spawning and may have had a survival advantage at a time when the sea was 'thick with predators' (Long, 2011, p. 37).

The initial *Materpiscis* discovery in 2008 was presented for a wider public through the journal *Nature*. Here, turning to more colloquial language, the discovery was headlined as 'the oldest pregnant mum', and the report concluded with an observation about the 'elaborate and violent courtship' behaviour of modern sharks (as the kin of placoderms) and the prurient suggestion that 'these findings [of viviparity] raise titillating speculation over placoderm sexual behaviour' (Dennis, 2008, p. 575). This practice of recasting scientific findings in anthropomorphic terms, with reference to courtship and titillation, foreshadows a tendency evident in relation to the unfolding discoveries about sexual reproduction in placoderms and sharks. In the textual presentation of these discoveries, we see the implicit continuation of that form of public pedagogy described in early feminist critiques of biological science. These critiques discussed the ways in which certain norms and values of human society are mapped onto the bodies and lives of animals, and then used as a mirror to reinforce as 'natural' a set of conservative sexual behaviours and hierarchies in humans (Haraway, 1978). As Crowther and Leith (1995) observed more than two decades ago, these practices, which underpin sociobiology, mean that 'human descriptions of the animal world are ultimately grounded in human perceptions of what human society is like' (p. 208). On this basis, scientific studies of animals, and the linguistic representation of these studies in popular science forums, serve as 'part of a wider public pedagogy governing human sexuality' (Crowther, 1999, p. 43).

Having discovered the pregnant placoderms to be the first vertebrate animals on Earth to have a complex form of sexual reproduction involving internal fertilisation, the next phase of research turned to the search for the placoderms' sexually differentiated reproductive organs (Long, Trinajstic & Johanson, 2009). Then in 2009 palaeontologists announced the discovery of a male placoderm clasper or sexual organ—specifically a long, articulated penis-like cartilage modified from a pelvic fin—which is similar to those found in living sharks (Ahlberg et al., 2009). While there had been much excitement around the discovery of the pregnant female placoderms, the identification of the placoderm clasper, or penis, was presented as 'an even more significant discovery' (*Nature* Video, 2009). In the video story of these discoveries, the Australian palaeontologist on the team, Dr John Long, claims that this finding 'is incredibly important because it's all about the origins of sex, sex in vertebrates, sex using copulation, males internally fertilising the females, and ah—that's intrinsically interesting I think to everyone on the planet' (*Nature* Video, 2009). Again, colloquial expressions are used to present this scientific discovery for a wider public. Long explains in the video: 'We have an expression that humans like to get a leg over, but these placoderms, actually like to get a leg in', thereby presenting a male-focused perspective and sustaining the titillating connotations that inhere in public pedagogies on this topic.

By 2011, the findings of placoderm internal fertilisation and live young had been further translated into a front-page story in the popular science magazine, *Scientific American*. The cover displays a large image of interlocking male and female sex symbols, with the male arrow piercing the female circle. As foregrounded in the editor's introduction, the story was pitched through an anthropomorphic lens, offering an insight into 'animals that had sex and gave birth the way we [humans] do' (DiChristina, 2011, p. 8). Under the title 'Dawn of the Deed', the report suggested that 'placoderms were the originators of intimate sexual reproduction', and that these findings 'are casting new light on the origin of our own [human] reproductive organs and other body parts' (Long, 2011, pp. 36–38). The article is replete with phrases that are integral to the discourses of evolution as the formative force in normative human sexuality:

> In the sexual equipment of these ancient placoderms we can thus see the earliest rudiments of our own reproductive system and other parts of our body and gain a clearer idea of how the anatomy changed over time to become what it is today. The paired pelvic fins that in placoderms permitted the males to deposit sperm into the females eventually gave rise to the genitalia and legs of tetrapods [including humans].
>
> (Long, 2011, p. 36)

Throughout this article, Long posits relationships between placoderm and human anatomy, and uses the language associated with human sexuality to describe placoderm reproduction. The placoderms were, for example, the 'originators of intimate sexual reproduction', giving rise to a 'sexual revolution' (Long, 2011, p. 38). The motivation for this shift from spawning to internal fertilisation is described in terms of 'getting in the mood', 'desire', and 'the hookup' (p. 39) and viewed primarily in terms of male agency. The text highlights the evolution of the human male penis from its origin in the male placoderm 'claspers' which are similar to those found on modern sharks. This focus on the development of male rather than female reproductive anatomy is crystalised in the evolutionary tree diagram, titled 'family ties', which illustrates the written description of 'the predominant form of reproduction for major vertebrate groups' (p. 38). The diagram shows placoderms at the ancestral base of the tree, with descendants on progressively higher upper branches: sharks, bony fishes, frogs, dinosaurs, birds, and eventually, on the highest branch, mammals. The exemplary mammal, the pinnacle of evolution at the top of the tree, is represented as a clothed human male. Despite the fact that the 'first hard evidence' of copulation was the discovery of the ancient mother fish, *Materpiscis,* and her kin (Long & Trinajstic, 2014), the remarkable female has been largely displaced from these revised narratives of reproductive evolution. The focus, at least in reports for a wider non-specialist audience, was now on the evolution of male sex organs.

In a later account of the placoderm male organ, published in the open access online website *The Conversation*, a further human-like metaphor and visual image are used. Here, Long and Trinajstic (2014) note that the 'bony placoderm claspers' were 'not rigidly fixed to the pelvic fin' and were 'able to rotate forwards, so the earliest sexual mating position was likely to have been a missionary one'. The accompanying image shows the female placoderm lying on what looks like a brown rock bed, in a supine horizontal position underneath a horizontal male. As I look at these images, I can't help but wonder: if they're floating, swimming, or suspended in the ocean, why are they lying in a bed with the female facing upwards like this, and why is the male shown on top? Does this depiction, legitimised through the discourses of science, simply narrativise an imagined past that secures traditional sexual mores?

In 2014 palaeontologists announced a further discovery. They had found, amongst an even older group of antiarch placoderms from around 385 million years ago, the earliest example of sexual dimorphism and distinct male and female sex organs in the fossil record. These newly discovered shark ancestors were named *Michrobrachius dicki*, after Scottish palaeontologist Robert Dick. The scientific report of this finding, which appeared in the journal *Nature* with the title 'Copulation in antiarch placoderms and the origin of gnathostome internal fertilization' (Long et al., 2015) displayed the linguistic hallmarks of a typically sober scientific article, with only a passing reference to a 'hypothetical mating position' and no explicit reference to the implications for human evolution.

This was markedly different from the way the *M. dicki* finding was reported in various science magazines and general news media; the differences were not only in the predictable shift in register, but also in the emphasis placed on sexual content. In *Australasian Science*, Long (Nov 2014) proposed that because of the position and shape of their bony genitalia, the antiarch placoderms mated 'from a sideways position', 'square-dance style' (p. 30), thus overturning the missionary position previously imagined for the placoderm. The article then turns to the significance for human evolution. Here we see another tree diagram showing the evolution of the male penis from a placoderm at the base to a human, modelled on Michelangelo's *David*, and with the smallest penis relative to body size, at the pinnacle. The triumphal diagram is captioned: 'A summary of the male intromittent sex organs, used in reproduction of vertebrates, from placoderms to us' (Long, 2014, p. 31). I can only assume 'us' refers to the generic human male.

In this move to the popular press, then, the focus shifted from fossil records of placoderms to the origins of human 'sex' (meaning copulation), the evolution of the male penis, and its ultimate manifestation in the human male. *National Geographic*, for example, announced the discovery of *M. dicki* under the headline 'Armored fish pioneered sex as you know it' and was peppered with sexual innuendo about 'The Act itself' (Switek, 2014). The *Washington Post* reporter, Terrence McCoy (2014) under the headline 'Scientists discover the awkward origins of sex', wrote that 'in the amorous world of the aptly-but-coincidentally named *M. dicki*, love was blind' and provided a quote from lead palaeontologist John Long, claiming that 'this was the earliest evidence of . . . sex that was fun'. The *Sydney Morning Herald* posted an account under the headline 'Ancient fish were first to have sex—but sideways', and quoted the lead palaeontologist as saying 'many of the traits and behaviours that first appeared in placoderms had travelled through the rest of evolution leading up to humans' (Phillips, 2014).

Hooking Up With Sharks

Research into modern shark reproduction is an important element in the struggle to conserve shark populations that are threatened by anthropogenic environmental damage and over-fishing. Studying shark mating systems is particularly important because their reproductive capacity is a key factor in ensuring long-term population sustainability. The current level of shark exploitation worldwide far exceeds the reproductive capacity of many species and has resulted in serious declines in some populations (Chapman et al., 2004). Sharks are particularly vulnerable to exploitation because, compared to other fishes, they have a very slow growth rate, late sexual maturity (often into their teens), low ovulation rate, long gestation period (up to two years), and relatively few young. They are also known to have sophisticated and complex reproductive behaviour (Pratt & Carrier, 2001). On the whole, however, and given the logistical problems associated with studying sharks in their natural environment, our understanding of shark mating systems is limited.

Despite the relative paucity of knowledge about shark reproduction, existing research suggests that polyandry and multiple paternity in litters is common in the majority of shark species (Lyons et al., 2017). Multiple mating by females—an activity common across vertebrate species—has been observed in many shark species, and many female sharks can store sperm, in some cases for over a year, opening the possibility of multiple paternity at a later date (Bryne & Avise, 2012; Fitzpatrick et al., 2012). At the same time, although female sharks are larger than males and often live in geographically sex-segregated groups, they may be discouraged from mating because of the serious injuries often inflicted by male sharks during mating encounters. Females can suffer severe lacerations and open wounds as a result of males biting the fins and flanks of females during mating; they may also suffer vaginal lacerations as a consequence of insertion of the male clasper. As Byrne and Avise (2012, p. 750) report, 'such occurrences render the female vulnerable during and after copulatory events to predation, blood loss, and infection; and, therefore, polyandrous behaviour may in effect decrease female fitness' to reproduce. Perhaps it's not surprising, then, that some female sharks may display evasive and uncooperative behaviours towards approaching males (Afonso et al., 2016; Pratt & Carrier, 2001). Yet Pratt and Carrier (2001) suggest that it is the female who, in most instances, initiates mating, or stimulates male interest with the release of pheromone chemicals into the water. Moreover, polyandry and multiple paternity may offer benefits to female sharks in terms of genetic diversity. To this end, female sharks have been shown to exercise 'cryptic female choice' with a variety of techniques for sperm selection and storage (for later fertilisation) after mating. These practices control sperm access to eggs, thereby increasing female control over paternity and reducing the possibility of producing offspring with any genetically unsuitable male (Chapman et al., 2004; Fitzpatrick et al., 2012; Lyons et al., 2017). Despite these intriguing dynamics of complex female agency, however, Lyons et al. (2017, p. 5604) observe that 'influences on multiple paternity from the female perspective generally go unconsidered', perhaps because such accounts don't support 'the primacy of the patriarchal macro-story' (Crowther, 1999, p. 53).

As with the media reporting on placoderm reproduction, the discourses, language, and style of media reports about shark reproductive behaviours differ significantly from those in scientific reports by demonstrating a far greater degree of anthropomorphism. A *National Geographic* blogger posits that the reason for the geographical sex segregation of mako sharks, for example, is 'one that many humans would relate to—sexual harassment' (Yong, 2009). A media release from the University of Illinois Chicago (2010) asks 'How do female whale sharks meet their perfect mates?' And in her report on sharks' reproductive behaviour, journalist Juliet Eilperin (2011) notes that male and female sharks 'don't intermingle frequently' and that 'when they do spend time with each other' their sexual behaviour is 'weird' and 'harsh'. From 'these revelations', Eilperin deduces 'a central fact about sharks':

> they cannot be anthropomorphized the way some other creatures have been. They are vastly different from humans in how they behave, and won't ever warm the hearts of the public the way penguins can.
>
> (Eilperin, 2011, p. 136)

And yet deeply anthropomorphic language shapes Eilperin's subsequent accounts of mating behaviour, where sharks are described as displaying 'intimate *dating* patterns': male sharks are '*suitors*' that can be seen '*stalking*' to improve 'their chances of *hooking up*' and multiple mating is called a '*gang-bang* phenomenon' with a 'social order [that] determines who *gets lucky*' (Eilperin, 2011, pp. 38–39, emphasis added). The invisible urge to anthropomorphise seems to be irresistible.

In a particularly risible example of sexualised anthropomorphism, a *National Geographic* YouTube video is bluntly titled 'Shark seduction' (Nat Geo Wild, 2013).[1] The video focuses on the mating behaviour of nurse sharks in the Florida Keys and the male narrator describes the sharks' activities in an exaggerated voice-over, producing a lewd and sleazy shark porn:

> Even at 14 feet and 230 pounds a female [nurse shark] is far more reminiscent of a femme fatale than a mild-mannered school nurse. No wonder the males get all riled up, and they're not shy about it. Most sharks are wary of having sex on tape: but not the nurse shark. . . . Warm water lagoons are the perfect place for nurse sharks. . . . Life couldn't be better. Unless you throw in a lot of sex. Females hang around the shallow area to be choosey about mates, and then head off to the bedroom, a particular area within the site. It all starts with a bite, and the female doesn't seem to mind one bit. Even if it's a success, the 20 to 50 nurse sharks in the coming litter will have at least six fathers. Sometimes a little promiscuity is good for a girl's gene pool.
>
> And so goes the shocking private lives of nurse sharks. Seems their behaviour with or without an audience is the same: it's all about sex.

The discourses shaping this wildlife video narration of sharks' sexual behaviour appears to have shifted from some decades earlier, when Rosalind Coward (1984, p. 210) observed the tendency in wildlife films to project conservative heteronormative ideologies about 'male aggression, bachelorhood, dominance, property, women's nesting instincts' onto other animals and then use these tropes to implicitly signal what is considered normal and natural in humans. Now, however, in the *National Geographic* shark sex drama the classic 'coy female' has been replaced by a new, more powerful model of hypersexualised female agency and availability. Perhaps, as Cynthia Chris (2006) suggests, cinematic images and interpretations of animal behaviour present the prevailing ideologies of human gender and sexuality, and in more recent times those ideologies have shifted to focus more intensely on a form of active female heterosexuality that nevertheless continues to support a patriarchal fantasy.

Jesus and Lonely Leonie

In contrast to the celebratory account of nurse shark heterosex, scientists have found that at least some female sharks display a remarkable ability to bear young without any genetic contribution from a male shark. The first scientific proof of this ability was announced by a team of scientists (Chapman et al., 2007) who studied the DNA of a baby hammerhead shark born in 2001 to a female that had been in captivity, in the absence of any male hammerheads, for three years. According to Eilperin (2011, p. 134), scientists nicknamed the baby shark *Jesus*, though an elementary understanding of genetic biology would suggest that this shark baby *Jesus* was a female. At the time, parthenogenesis or 'virgin birth' had been documented in all jawed vertebrate lineages except for mammals and cartilaginous fishes (sharks, rays, and chimera). But amongst sharks, the birth of baby sharks in the absence of a male shark had formerly been attributed to the ability of females to store male sperm for later use. Reports of this first documented case of true parthenogenesis were published for the readership of *Science Daily*, a popular science news website, under the heading 'No sex please, we're female sharks' (Queen's University Belfast, 2007), reflecting the more traditional anthropomorphic discourse of sexually modest females (Crowther, 1995, 1999).

Scientists at the time warned that parthenogenesis was not a positive strategy for shark species because any offspring carried only the mother's DNA and missed out on the genetic diversity available from the paternal side.

Nevertheless, more instances of virgin birth in captivity were confirmed in the years since the initial proof of the female shark's ability to reproduce without a male mate. These included a case in which a female bamboo shark produced multiple vigorous offspring that survived at least five years (Feldheim et al., 2010), and a case where a female zebra or leopard shark, confined in a Dubai hotel pool, produced offspring annually over a four-year period (Choi, 2012). When investigating another possible case of virgin birth in 2014, scientists in California tested the offspring of a female bamboo shark that had been isolated from males for a few years. In this case, they found the pup had been produced from the mother's egg and male sperm she had stored for nearly four years (Bernal et al., 2015). Not a case of parthenogenesis, but a remarkable strategy for a female shark to prolong her fertility in the absence of a male shark and offer hope for maintaining genetic diversity.

When a female zebra shark named Leonie reproduced by virgin birth in Australia in 2016, scientific reports emphasised that this was the first documented case of a female shark switching from sexual to asexual reproduction (Dudgeon et al., 2017). Another zebra shark in the same enclosure had also reproduced parthenogenically but without any prior mating experience. Although some scientists had argued that parthenogenesis was simply an accidental reproductive error rather than an adaptive strategy (Van der Kooi & Schwander, 2015), the zebra shark findings suggested that female sharks can flexibly adapt their reproductive strategy to changing environmental circumstances (Dudgeon et al., 2017, p. 3).

While the standard scientific reports of Leonie's feat were predictably sober, media accounts of the event were more frequent and far more florid than those appearing in the wake of previous cases of parthenogenesis. They illustrate a particular style of gendered anthropomorphic discourses that seems to have flourished with the rise of social media and the availability of web-based popular science publishing platforms. 'Ladies, hold on to your hats' was the opening line from the *National Geographic* (Little, 2017), followed by a faux coy comment that this was the first time that scientists had seen this 'behavior in a shark that wasn't, ahem, a virgin' (para. 2). 'Lonely leopard shark learns to reproduce by herself' was the headline in online media site *New Atlas* (Irving, 2017). In the *New Scientist*, Klein (2017) opened with the line 'Who needs men? A female shark separated from her long-term mate has developed the ability to have babies on her own'. Klein went on to describe how 'Leonie . . . met her partner in an aquarium in Townsville', speculating that she had been 'storing sperm from her ex'. In an item for Australia's public broadcaster, *ABC News*, Briggs (2017) reported an observation from the aquarium's senior aquarist: 'People are amazed when we tell them we have leopard sharks that don't need males, a lot of the males get a bit frightened because they think "oh no, we're becoming obsolete!"' Katie Russell (2017), reporting for the online UK media site, *The Debrief*, presented arguably the most colourful account, with the headline 'Lonely female shark fights the patriarchy and gets pregnant without partner', and the subheading 'Meet the single mum shark who don't need no man'. Russell continues:

> Three years ago, a young female named Leonie was abandoned by her partner. He left without a goodbye, not even to their offspring. It's a story many of us can relate to, but with one key difference: Leonie is a shark.
>
> How did Leonie deal with this news? Did she go into a Bridget Jones-style slump and eat nothing but the shark equivalent of Ben & Jerry's for the rest of her life? Absolutely not. Instead, this leopard shark has defied all the odds and given birth again, despite being celibate for three years.

Russell concluded her story with a quote from the television programme *Grey's Anatomy*: 'It's amazing how much you get done without a penis'.

It's easy to see, in these examples, how discourses of human sexuality are projected onto other animals in the course of narrating animal behaviours. In the case of Leonie, those projections can tell a range of contradictory stories: about female loneliness without a male partner; about the questionable value of female virginity; about female agency and liberation without a male partner; about male callousness in sexual relationships; about the redundancy of males in processes of reproduction. From the instances discussed here it seems that these discourses, translated from those emerging in the natural sciences, have become more hyperbolic and human-centric through the work of social news media. As with the previous stories of shark mating, the range of discourses used in accounts of parthenogenesis have expanded from those observed in pre-internet decades, perhaps reflecting the effects of third wave feminism. With the rise of social media and popular online news outlets, these gendered anthropomorphic discourses now range across a spectrum from the 'coy female' (no sex please) and 'compulsory heterosexuality' (lonely Leonie) to the 'crisis of masculinity' (frightened, obsolete males) and the sexualised agency of single, liberated females (getting the job done without a penis).

Tracking Sharks and Media Stars

One of the reasons that sharks remain such enigmatic creatures is that humans have found them so difficult to research. Until recently, studying the behaviour and movements of sharks and other highly migratory marine species has been difficult due to the challenges of working in aquatic environments. In recent years, however, advances in DNA analysis and a variety of electronic tagging and tracking tools (including GPS, sensors, mini-cameras), together with sophisticated statistical and analytical techniques, have provided increased opportunities to remotely study individual sharks, trace their movements and residency patterns, identify their use of habitats for feeding or giving birth, assess their movements in relation to environmental data, including temperature changes, salt concentrations, water depth, moon phases and so on, and evaluate certain threats they may face in the environments in which they swim (Costa, Breed & Robinson, 2012).

More specifically, these technologies are said to provide information to assist conservation of endangered species such as the great white shark, increasing our knowledge about where they go, what they do, and which habitats are critical for their survival. With tagging and tracking, Peschera (2016, p. 9) argues that animal life is rendered 'transparent and tangible', that animals regarded as dangerous to humans can be freed from 'the snare of misrepresentation', allowing each to 'turn back into a normal animal'. More broadly, Peschera celebrates the ways in which digital technologies and tracking can open a 'new dialogue between humans and nature' (p. 9) and re-establish our connection to the animal kingdom. Yet the ability of humans to perceive the natural world other than through the lens of our deeply entrenched discursive expectations may be limited. It seems unrealistic, then, to expect a 'new language' and a new liberation, for either human or non-human animals, to arise from the introduction of new digital technologies for animal surveillance.

By 2011, the great white shark, *Caracharodon carcharias*, had become the most heavily satellite-tracked shark species (Hammerschlag, Gallagher & Lazarre, 2011), yielding major insights into their long-range migratory patterns, with some sharks showing transoceanic migrations of over 30,000 km (Lee, 2014). Yet the reasons for these long migrations is still unknown; possibilities are suggested but empirical evidence is lacking.

Despite the absence of empirical data, ocean scientists who were keen to investigate sharks' migratory motivations have tended to rely, at least in part, on the projection of human assumptions and generalised theoretical models. In the case of great white sharks, one team of scientists (Pardini et al., 2001) analysed DNA data from two distinct shark populations—one from South African waters, the other from Australian and New Zealand waters—with the aim of investigating migration patterns between these two populations on opposite sides of the Indian Ocean. On the basis of a limited number of genetic tests, the scientists deduced that only some of the sharks made the long transoceanic migration; they suggested that those were 'probably' the 'roving' male sharks, and that the 'non-roving' female sharks remained in their own home waters. These findings were summarised conclusively as follows: 'Here we use genetic methods to show that dispersal of *C. carcharias* is sex-biased, with philopatric (non-roving) females and roving males' (Pardini et al., 2001, p. 139). And yet they admit that there was 'no direct evidence for this idea' (p. 139), apart from other reports of sex-differentiated habitat use and migration.

Several years later, however, a satellite tracking study of the same great white shark populations contradicted previous ideas that females stayed home while males undertook long transoceanic migrations (Bonfil et al., 2005). This study tagged and tracked sharks off the South African coast and analysed their complex spatial dynamics. The team identified a female shark who completed the migration across the entire Indian Ocean from South Africa to Australia and return—'the fastest transoceanic return migration recorded among marine fauna'—showing remarkable navigation skills and taking just nine months to complete a circuit of more than 20,000 km (Bonfil et al., 2005, p. 101). While the data collected in the study do not provide a full understanding of the way the two populations are connected, these scientists suggest that transoceanic migration is more likely to be undertaken by South African *female* sharks travelling across the ocean, mating with white sharks in the Australian population, and returning to give birth in South Africa, thereby overturning previous assumptions based on traditional patriarchal notions of female passivity and domesticity.

Another set of studies has investigated populations of great white sharks in the northeastern Pacific. In one study (Jorgensen et al., 2010, 2012), a team of scientists tracked a population of sharks and found that they moved in a highly structured seasonal migratory cycle between the California coast, the Hawaiian archipelago, and a site deep in the northeastern Pacific known as the 'White Shark Café'. The causes and consequences of the migration were unknown, but speculation centred on the importance of the Café for feeding and mating. At one specific site within the Café zone, electronic tags recorded a strange pattern of energetic, vertical deep-sea diving by male sharks, descending to a depth of around 400 metres up to 150 times per day (Jorgensen et al., 2010). Although female sharks occasionally visited the Café waters, they were more widely dispersed across the site and tended not to linger where the males were gathered. In the absence of any direct evidence of mating at any location in the migration route, the scientists proposed that the Café may function primarily as a mating site, and interpreted the diving as a ritualised male courtship display to attract the attention of female sharks. Here again, scientific assumptions about animal behaviour appear to be shaped by a conservative 'patriarchal macro-story' (Crowther, 1999, p. 53) that would attribute competitive courtship behaviour to male sharks and discriminating passivity to female sharks.

However, the hypothesis of deep diving as a courtship ritual was contradicted by a subsequent study. In this investigation, improved tagging batteries were used to track female white sharks over a two-year migration cycle, a pattern that contrasts with the annual migration cycle of males (Domeier & Nasby-Lucas, 2013). Tracking showed that females spent little time in the Café zone, and based on the female sharks' reproductive cycle Domeier and Nasby-Lucas (2013) hypothesised that the sharks were more likely to be mating near the onshore locations rather than in the offshore White Shark Café. As Domeier observed 'males and females have very different habits . . . they are rarely in the same place at the same time' (cited in Giordiani, 2013). Moreover, Domeier and Nasby-Lucas (2013) noted that sharks have never been known to participate in 'lek-like mating systems', a term that refers to the 'gathering of males at a traditional site for the purpose of ritualized courtship display' and, in turn, the selection by females of a 'specific male for mating' (p. 6). These contradictory findings indicate the fragility of conservative anthropomorphic models when imposed on one group of animals by another.

Similarly, anthropomorphic gendered projections onto non-human bodies can be seen in the reporting of a study of whale shark migration. In this case, one scientific study (Andrzejaczek et al., 2016) used photo-identification to assess the connectedness of five whale shark population sites across the Indian Ocean, including one site at Ningaloo Reef off the coast of Western Australia. At each gathering site a much higher proportion of juvenile male whale sharks was found relative to females, and these five shark populations remained quite distinct. The study reported that once these juvenile whale sharks leave the gathering sites their individual movements are largely unknown due to the difficulty of long-range tracking in deep oceans.

While the original journal article reported these findings in matter-of-fact detail, the accompanying media statement presented the findings through the lens of an anthropomorphic gendered narrative. Under the heading 'Teenage male whale sharks don't want to leave home', the authors claimed that they were 'surprised to discover that the male juveniles didn't seem to venture too far from home' (Stacey, Andrzejaczek & Meekan, 2016, para. 1). These sharks are described in the media statement as 'male teenagers' and 'homebodies' (para. 12), with the authors remarking that some of the males have been sighted in a particular location 'for 19 years and have even matured' (para. 9). As far the human stereotype goes, it is the female human who is— and should be—a 'homebody'. In the reporting of the sharks' behaviour, the juvenile males are ridiculed for their habit of staying with their own 'home' population and thereby failing to conform with traditional human gender expectations. At the core of the media announcement, we see an interpretation of shark behaviour through the lens of naturalised sexist hierarchies.

The scientific 'surprise' lies in the disruption of a conservative stereotype that distinguishes adventurous males from passive females, and a reversal of the life-trajectory stereotype wherein young males move away from a family of origin, and females remain.

As an offshoot of this scientific technology, shark tracking has been popularised through social media platforms, in particular through the controversial work of OCEARCH, an organisation funded by corporate sponsorship that provides an ocean vessel to be used by shark research teams as a roving field station. The vessel is owned by a former reality-TV host, Chris Fischer, and was previously used as a 'travelling TV set' for the capture and filming of live great white sharks. The original film footage, packaged under macho titles such as '*Shark Men*' and '*Shark Wranglers*', was sold for broadcast on the National Geographic and History Channels (Streep, 2015).

Faltering television ratings led the OCEARCH vessel's owners to find a new approach to making money from shark wrangling. The vessel now captures and tags sharks in order to generate open-source tracking data which, in turn, has been made widely accessible through its translation into visual images on the OCEARCH website. The visual images are produced by dots that appear on a digital map each time a shark surfaces and the shark's transmitter 'pings' its location to a satellite. Each of the sharks is given a name by the research team—a move that is said to increase human interest in the sharks—and viewers can read information about each shark by clicking on the dots and can track where each shark has been since it was tagged. Several of the tagged sharks—including three female great whites—Mary Lee, Katherine, and Lydia—became social media celebrities when they were tagged and tracked online by thousands of people using the OCEARCH Global Shark Tracker app (Pulver, 2016). Followers of Katherine, for example, were so keen on seeing her status and whereabouts that in 2014 visitors to the OCEARCH website were crashing the research site's servers (Mearian, 2014).

A further translation of the sharks' travels emerged when their mapped data were taken up by people using Instagram and Twitter to give a 'voice' to the tagged sharks. The Twitter account, @MaryLeeShark, was created by a shark fan and had attracted 129K followers by the time her tag stopped pinging in 2017. Her media celebrity led to Mary Lee being named 'the most famous shark since Jaws' (Leber, 2018, para. 1). Other accounts, including @Shark_Katherine and @RockStarLydia created and launched by OCEARCH, have also attracted thousands of followers. Interviews with two of the people who are behind the shark 'voices' tell a similar story of the conversion they experienced as a result of their shark ventriloquism, finding that their initial horror of sharks was transformed into empathy and understanding about the role of sharks in healthy oceans (Landers, 2017; Leber, 2018).

Publicity generated by the OCEARCH project is couched in the discourses of shark conservation. In developing social media platforms to allow a global audience to track the sharks, the research team aims for a shark 're-brand' (Crosby, 2017, para. 4) that will replace the fears and misconceptions surrounding sharks with an interest in their unique lives and a concern for their endangered status (Marcelo, 2015). According to Mearian (2015, para. 30), the scientists 'believe their work has been critical to changing the public attitude toward one of the ocean's apex predators'. As the OCEARCH founder Chris Fischer points out, prior to the project of shark tracking on this scale, the only stories published about sharks in news media were reports of *Jaws*-like attacks on people. The new data and media platforms, together with giving each shark a name, purportedly allow this narrative of fear to be replaced by a different sort of affective interest in sharks and their behaviours (Crosby, 2017). Nevertheless, changing people's ingrained perceptions of sharks in the waters where people swim and surf is unlikely to be so easily achieved, and while mainstream media now publishes a mixture of stories about shark attacks and shark conservation—such as those that followed the 2015 Mick Fanning shark encounter—the headline images and texts are still dominated by fear-inducing discourses symbolised in images of the body and teeth of the shark .

The sophisticated electronic tagging and tracking technologies deployed by bodies such as OCEARCH have been hailed by some scholars as opening up new relationships between humans and animals. In one celebratory assessment, these revolutionary technologies are said to 'allow animals to communicate [with us] autonomously', affording a 'realistic impression of nature' that overcomes the barriers formed by earlier ideological and theoretical modelling and representation (Peschera, 2016, p. 47). But this seems a rather naïve assessment, one that overlooks the embodied entanglements occurring between sharks and humans and enabled by the tagging and tracking technologies. In a more critical evaluation of this process, the operations of the OCEARCH team have been labelled an 'adrenalized' and 'swashbuckling brand of research', a description that seems apt when one views the footage of the crew, journalists, filmmakers, and scientists, most (if not all) of whom are men keen to 'get their hands on a live white shark', (OCEARCH owner, Chris Fischer, quoted in Streep, 2015). The hunting and capture, carried out under the auspice of an owner driven by personal ambition and bombast, sounds little different from the masculinised ritual of wildlife hunting that is celebrated by big game fishermen in their competition to slaughter the largest female sharks (male sharks being smaller) despite their endangered status (Howard, 2013). In the case of OCEARCH, the process of hooking and hauling the sharks out of the water, combined with the intense drilling, bolting, tagging, sampling, and measuring operations, have themselves been criticised as highly invasive, brutal, and traumatising—even fatal—for the sharks (Kretzmann, 2012; Streep, 2015).

More broadly, and in the context of an otherwise celebratory representation of electronic animal surveillance, Peschera (2016) sounds some words of warning about the impact of tracking technologies for animal lives, and for human–animal relationships. Although these technologies promise a 'newfound closeness' between human and non-human animals, Peschera (2016, p. 11) laments that 'nature' and the wonderful 'chaos of wilderness' will be radically changed as a consequence of human intrusion and surveillance:

> The thicket will be digitally cleared. Nature, defined as the untouched in the Western imagination, will not only be touched, but penetrated . . . the natural world remaining after this era will be a desecrated, denuded one. . . . The Animal Internet is turning nature into a system controlled, if not created, by humans.
>
> (Peschera, 2016, p. 11)

In an era where life can be translated digitally and displayed on a screen, debate about 'big data' has usually focussed on the degree to which humans will tolerate surveillance and monitoring controlled by corporate and government interests. Humans have pushed back to protect themselves against control and surveillance of this sort. But with the Animal Internet 'humans will push their way deep into the lives of animals; they will break open their "personal space" . . . the prospect of a *transparent nature* seems like an expansion of the digital war zone' (Peschera, 2016, p. 13, emphasis in original).

The Questionable Value of Scientific Knowledge

The stories told in this chapter reveal just a few of the ways in which science has revealed new knowledge about living sharks and their ancient ancestors. Yet the stories leave me with a strange sense of unease and loss. Are humans on scientific quests continuing on from an earlier age of imperial exploration, 'discovery', and colonisation of the planet and her varied inhabitants? As with those earlier incarnations, is this a masculinised endeavour to locate and map, dissect, and analyse all the components of life in the more-than-human world, rendering this life in a set of multimodal human languages?

There seems little doubt that these scientific exploits have revealed more, in a technical sense, than we previously knew about sharks and their observable habits. But the extent to which this knowledge has supported conservation measures, or transformed human habits of greed and destruction, is unclear.

Note

1. *Shark seduction.* Available at: www.youtube.com/watch?v=34kpy3HB3RQ

6 Shark Fantasy

Shark Movie Monsters

No survey of the discourses, representations, and fleshy realities of sharks would be complete without mention of Steven Spielberg's movie *Jaws*, based on Peter Benchley's book of the same name. Despite celebrating its 40th birthday in 2015, the story and imagery of *Jaws* continues to resonate with our collective understanding of sharks because the movie carries within it a complex tangle of social, cultural, political traditions.

The plot of *Jaws* is, on the surface, deceptively simple. One summer, in the small seaside town of Amity on Long Island—all toy-bright and picket-fence pretty—tranquility is disrupted by the arrival of a rogue shark which kills several people. The town's mayor and business folk are reluctant to close the beach and lose the tourist trade on which they depend. Panic mounts as the shark wreaks havoc. Eventually three men—Brody the timid policeman, Hooper the wealthy young out-of-town oceanographer, and Quint the rugged old salt—set out on a boat to hunt the shark. In the ensuing struggle, Quint is slain by the shark monster, Hooper disappears into the ocean, and Brody overcomes his water-phobic fears and achieves a hero's victory when he manages to shoot a large bomb-shaped weapon into the shark's mouth. The town rejoices at the return of their saviour, together with the revived Hooper.

Despite this seeming simplicity, *Jaws* has been the object of countless critical interpretations since its release in 1975. It represents something of a gravitational centre for meanings associated with the figure and body of the shark, drawing meaning from the links between characters' narratives and broader social, cultural, economic, historical, and political phenomena and events. The movie also functions as a powerful form of public pedagogy (Giroux, 2008) that draws on the formal and affective qualities of film to reproduce, amplify, and circulate particular understandings of and responses to sharks.

In one prominent analytical tradition, *Jaws* represents 'the definitive articulation of a myth' (Quirke, 2002, p. 6), a rendition of the archetypal narrative known as 'Overcoming the Monster' (Booker, 2004). This is a narrative retold over centuries, appearing in folk tales, poems, novels, and movies. The ravenous ocean-dwelling sea monster must be slain by the Greek hero Perseus in order to rescue the beautiful virgin princess, Andromeda. In the 8th century story of *Beowulf*, a monster from the deep attacked and dismembered villagers in a peaceful seaside community until it was finally slain by a brave hero. In the 19th century, the monster appeared in the form of a white whale in *Moby Dick*, a creature that troubled Captain Ahab and became the target for his expression of an obsessive, vengeful masculinity. In the movie trailer for *Jaws*, the fear induced by this ancient archetype is borne out in the sonorous, dramatic voice-over:

There is a creature alive today that has survived millions of years of evolution without change, without passion, and without logic. It lives to kill; a mindless, eating machine. It will attack and devour anything. It is as if God created the devil and gave him . . . *Jaws*. None of man's fantasies of evil can compare with the reality . . . of *Jaws*.

Yet this analysis leaves us asking: *who, or what, is the monster*? And, of course, the answer depends on one's standpoint, context, and perspective.

The movie was originally released at a point in time when the U.S. military alliance suffered its final defeat in the war against North Vietnam and when second-wave feminism had mounted a significant challenge to male dominance and heteronormative traditions. Indeed, the emergence of '*Jaws* hysteria' at a time of social upheaval is, according to Crawford (2008, p. 75), no coincidence: shark-related panic has become a popular ploy by the media to turn public attention away from more significant human-centred catastrophes, including the ravages of war. From the point of view of the U.S. alliance, the distinctive anxieties and trauma of the Vietnam war called for a 'therapeutic intervention' to heal a 'damaged American pride', a response provided by the reassuring narrative of *Jaws* in which the monstrous but elusive enemy is eventually tracked down and annihilated through the actions of three brave men (Torry, 1993, p. 33).

But Vietnam was not the only social and political crisis of the times. Biskind (1975), for example, reads the movie as an allegory for the Watergate scandal, proposing that the Amity town mayor, Vaughn, is a Nixon-like figure, bent on covering up the initial shark attack in order to protect his commercial interests. The OPEC oil crisis, the cold war, the atomic bomb, drugs, hippies, youthful protest, and social change in the West were also key features of the times and each has been associated with metaphorical meanings in the movie.

The 1970s was also an era of heightened environmental consciousness. At a time when environmentalists and animal rights activists called for people to respect the planet and protect natural habitats, Drummond (1996, pp. 218–219) suggests that *Jaws* gave audiences a release from shame and guilt, a scapegoat in the form of '*an animal to hate*' and, in the destructive ending, a 'solution to the mounting problems we face in sharing the earth with other living creatures'. In this sense, *Jaws* is typical of animal horror movies that invoke our fear of non-human creatures and justify the degradation of nature more broadly (Gregersdotter, Höglund & Hållén, 2015), all of which, in turn, plays on a fantasy separation between human culture and untamed nature that is fundamental to modernity (Latour, 1993; Armstrong, 2002). This fantasy of man-against-monster soon bled into reality when an unrealistic fear of sharks, provoked by *Jaws*, mobilised a 'collective testosterone rush' that made it 'sexy to go catch sharks', legitimated competitive shark-hunting expeditions, and contributed to the decimation of vulnerable shark populations in critical ocean habitats (Burgess, cited in Choi, 2010). Yet ironically, the movie also prompted an increase in scientific research into, and understanding of, sharks' biology, behaviour, and crucial importance in healthy ocean ecologies (Francis, 2011).

Representing the Shark as the Other

While Vietnam, Watergate, and other 1970s crises position the movie in a specific historical moment, it is the deeper social, cultural, and political meanings in the movie that outlive these temporal crises. The ongoing appeal of the movie, according to most analyses, lies in the meaning of Otherness attached to the shark as a 'dark and ungraspable presence that lurks beneath the surface of the ocean and breaks through to unsettle hegemonic culture' (Hamscha, 2013, p. 220). In this sense, the figure of the monstrous shark arises from our deepest subconscious, where our inner demons dwell (Bowles, 1976), embodying 'ideologically reviled human attributes, made radically Other, to be expunged' (Morris, 2007, p. 49). The only way to counter this disruptive intruder and to keep the dominant cultural structure intact is to kill the shark and restore the illusion of an idyllic, blameless, and unified society (Hamscha, 2013).

For Žižek (2012), too, the key to understanding the meaning of the shark in *Jaws* lies in its function as the Other, with the shark as an empty signifier designed to contain a multitude of social fears. Those fears might be of foreign invaders, natural disasters, or the evil military–industrial alliance, entities that can all be condensed in the body of the shark attacking people at their beachside holiday. As an example, Žižek explains the function of the shark through a comparison with Nazi Germany, where the multitude of internal social instabilities inherent in capitalism were resolved through an ideological narrative that blamed those instabilities on the foreign intruder, the Jew.

> The same operation as with the shark: you have a multitude of fears, and this multitude confuses you, you simply don't know what's the meaning of all this confusion. So you replace this multitude with one single figure, the Jew, and everything becomes clear. To maintain the social order, you need a single figure, and this figure can mobilise us. The Other, as someone who tries to steal something of *ours*, who tries to disturb *our* way of life.
>
> (Žižek, 2012)

In a similar vein, Fredric Jameson (1979) described the shark in *Jaws* as a polysemous symbol, capable of absorbing historical, social, and organic anxieties about the invasive Other, or about birth, copulation, and death, and the folding of these back into apparently natural fears about the killer shark. Those fears were thus 'both expressed and contained in what looks like a conflict with other forms of biological existence' (Jameson, 1979, p. 142), and so the eventual defeat of the shark was a means of ensuring the Utopian restitution of social order. Jameson, however, chooses to analyse the movie through a Marxist lens, and sees the shark in *Jaws* as a mass media decoy which draws attention away from a deeper ideological struggle played out between the male protagonists who represent different figures in the age of advanced capitalism. He reads the death of the older shark hunter, Quint, as the death of an old-fashioned American enterprise based on small business and wartime sacrifice. In the figures of Brody, the policeman, and Hooper, the young technocratic oceanographer, Jameson reads a new, triumphant alliance between the forces of law and order (Brody) and the new technocracy of multinational corporations (Hooper), a 'spurious kind of fraternity in which the viewer rejoices without understanding that he or she is excluded from it' (Jameson, 1979, p. 144). In Jameson's analysis, then, we lose sight of the central figure of the shark who slips away in the glare of battle between these men.

Vagina Dentata

Perhaps the most revealing, enduring, and abundant analyses of *Jaws* are those critical accounts that view the movie through the lens of human gender identity and sexuality. Several such analyses appeared in the years

following the movie's release, no doubt inspired by second-wave feminism. Biskind (1975) for example, reads the movie as an extended sexual
fantasy featuring the shark as a giant phallus, while for Rubey (1976), the
shark 'reflects a disguised hatred of women and the preoccupation of society with sadistic sexuality' (para 2). This focus on sadistic sexual connotations is foregrounded in the opening scenes of the movie where we meet the
first *Jaws* victim, a carefree, bohemian, adventurous young blonde woman,
Chrissie Watkins, at a night-time beach party. Chrissie leads an admiring
young man away from the fireside group, and he pursues her as she runs
off over the sand dunes, discarding her clothes along the way. She enters
the water naked under moonlight, he falls down drunk on the sandy shore
and passes out. The camera shifts to the dark water, viewing Chrissie's
naked body from below, loosely floating and unaware of the approaching
danger. We hear the throbbing, rhythmic score that heralds the approach
of the shark, a monstrous beast intent on conquering and consuming her.
Torture ensues, Chrissie's body writhes in pain, or is it ecstasy? In any
case, the young woman is the victim and the marauding shark assaults her
violently, sexually, and in her agonised visage Rubey (1976) sees 'a frightening imitation of orgasm'. She is powerless, the shark is all powerful. In
this scene, Biskind (1975, para 8–9) interprets the shark as a metaphor for
'the young man's sexual passion, a greatly enlarged, marauding penis',
and sees the attack as punishment for the young woman's 'sexual freedom
and forwardness'. Other critics agree that this is a scene of violent rape,
inflicted on a bold girl, a wicked and wild sea siren (Caputi, 1978; Quirke,
2002). As the narrative unfolds there are more fatal attacks, highlighting
the inability of the town's menfolk to address the threat and raising the
spectre of the shark as a symbol of impotence and castration. The turmoil
eventually prompts a quest by the three male heroes, each equipped with
an appropriate phallus-shaped weapon, to reassert masculine control and
restore moral and sexual order.

An alternative psychosexual reading sees the movie as the 'ritual retelling of an essential patriarchal myth' in which the shark, as the primordial
female, the *Magna Mater* in the form of a sea goddess/monster, must be
slain by the holy trinity of male heroes—Quint the father, and the two sons
Brody and Hooper—in order to reaffirm the patriarchal social order (Caputi,
1978, p. 305). The initial attack on Chrissie Watkins is, according to Caputi,
a 'carefully constructed form of subliminal cinematic rape' and murder
(p. 319), perpetrated not by the shark but by the young man who pursues
her across the sand dunes. In response, the archetypal, revenging guardian
spirit, taking the form of the marauding shark, wreaks revenge throughout the rest of the movie by attacking only males. The ocean itself, the
primal womb and source of life where desire, union, and dismemberment

take place, is the mythic symbol of the unconscious, 'the realm of thought and creativity which remains a wilderness, beyond the colonizing grasp of patriarchal socialization' (p. 323). With the ultimate destruction of the she-shark, however, the purpose of the movie, and other myths of this genre, is fulfilled: to inculcate fear and hatred for the female, and thereby justify her annihilation.

In Caputi's reading, the fear of sharks is associated with patriarchal fear of untamed female power and the female body. The threat posed by the she-shark centres in particular on the threat of castration symbolised in the image of the shark's open mouth—the creatures are 'all mouth' (Quirke, 2002, p. 30)—as a representation of the *vagina dentata* or vagina with teeth. Here, the gaping jaws are the provocation for phallic panic, the dread and horror aroused by the uncanny alignment of woman, the animal, and death (Creed, 1993). The shark has become the rapacious, uncontained female lover who consumes and incorporates her mate, castrating or killing him in the process (Grosz, 1995, p. 282). This imagery of *vagina dentata* indicates, for Harrington (2018), a deep unease with women's sexuality and reflects 'negative attitudes towards the vagina in contemporary culture that are put to work to actively repudiate any power inherent in the feminine' (p. 56). In the *Jaws* movie, we see Quint, as the symbol of traditional, vengeful, masculinity, swallowed up in the mouth of the shark, in the monstrous *vagina dentata*, where lurks the fear of male dismemberment.[1] Quint's version of patriarchal civilisation can be restored only after the female is vanquished. In the movie this resolution comes about when Matt Brody, the troubled police chief, restores his own masculine potency by firing an explosive phallus-shaped cylinder into the shark's gaping mouth.[2]

Shark Sequels

In later years, continuing renditions of the shark-monster movie have failed to live up to the complex sociopolitical, gendered, and sexualised imagery of *Jaws*.

By some counts, more than 70 movies about sharks have been made for cinema and television since the early 1900s (Brown, 2016). The meanings they project onto the body of the shark are evident in titles such as *White Death* (1936), *Monster Shark* (1984), *Deep Blood* (1989), *Raging Sharks* (2005), *Shark Killer* (2015), *Zombie Shark* (2015), and *Toxic Shark* (2017). Horror movies and thrillers such as *Deep Blue Sea* (1999), *Shark Night 3D* (2011), *The Shallows* (2016), and even the satirical *Sharkenstein* (2016) and *Sharknado* sharksploitation series (2013–2018), are typical of the post-*Jaws* shark-monster genre and echo many of the sharkly tropes established in Spielberg's 1975 blockbuster. In each of these movies, the shark can be read as a floating signifier for the projection of repressed human fears. In the case of *Deep Blue Sea*, these are fears about xenotransplantation and genetically engineered animals. In the *Sharknado* movies we see a farcical take on fears about the catastrophic consequences of climate change, while movies such as *Shark Night 3D* centre on concerns with post-teen sexuality and latent rape fantasies. At the same time, the sharks in each of these movies can also been seen as creatures to be feared in their actual physical presence, as monsters set on devouring hapless humans.

The shark-monster theme is explored from a slightly different angle in the 2011 Australian movie, *The Reef*, which follows the fate of a group of friends sailing from Australia to Indonesia when their yacht strikes a reef and capsizes. The friends swim through open water in the hope of reaching land, but one by one they are devoured by sharks. Based on a true story, the movie aims for documentary-like naturalism and displays the ocean as a frightening, featureless expanse that invokes the postcolonial anxieties of a settler culture, lost, and out of place in an ancient land. Below the watery surface, deadly sharks lurk as a shadowy, invisible, Otherness, their presence tapping into primal human fears of mortality and cannibalism.

In Fuchs' (2015) reading of *The Reef*, this movie is an ecocritical text that challenges the notion of human mastery over nature and emphasises the subjection of humans to an unknowable natural environment. In this rendition, and in contrast to the movie *Jaws*, the sharks survive their encounter with the human creatures, thereby providing an ecological perspective that decentres the human from an imagined position at the top a natural hierarchy. In *The Reef*, then, the conventional representation of the shark-as-monster again remains largely undisturbed and unquestioned. Yet Fuchs' analysis overlooks the ways in which the movie narrative also highlights a traditional set of normative heterosexual relationships amongst a cast of vulnerable, frightened young women and courageous men whose strategies and masculine determination drive the action. In the movie's concluding scenes, the shark facilitates the performance of a romantic tragedy as the hero valiantly sacrifices his own life to save his female love-interest. From this perspective, it seems the sharks have no role other than to provoke a drama of human challenges and provide the opportunity to strengthen human stereotypes. Although the sharks are neither hunted nor killed, they remain in their allotted place as the monstrous, abject Other.

Indeed, each of these shark movies, despite their differences, regurgitates predictable heterosexual norms and clichés. Young, physically attractive female movie stars invariably appear as sexualised objects of phallocentric fantasy and the voyeuristic, often sadistic, male gaze; these young bodies are tormented by an often invisible yet ever-present shark, always lurking and watching, ready to attack. In a recent iteration, *The Shallows* (2016) focuses on an athletic young female actor who loses her surfboard and is unable to swim to shore while a menacing great white shark circles and attacks, causing her to shed most of her surfing gear except for a tiny bikini. This is, in the words of film critic Roger Ebert (2016) 'a one-woman show' that puts the female lead 'on a jagged rocky pedestal and worships her', with the camera trained on her agile body and offering many shots in which her 'posterior is so lovingly scrutinized'. This form of sexual objectification of the female stars is foregrounded in the majority of shark movie posters where we see the women's bodies presented, in the role of shark attack victim, for voyeuristic enjoyment.[3]

Retelling *Jaws*

Inspiration for a feminist and ecosensitive retelling of the woman-and-beast narrative is difficult to find within the world of shark movies. In these, the more traditional tropes and stereotyped narratives persist, with limited variations on patriarchal heterosexual hierarchies (human female victim and male hero) and a greater or lesser (but always present) focus on the horror of being dismembered and eaten by a voracious marauding shark. Yet beyond this visual focus on the female body, it is the abiding relationship between the wily woman and the powerful shark that intrigues me. How can we imagine their relationship differently? How can we celebrate their intertwined human–shark agencies, creativities, potentialities, and resistance to domination?

Throughout the history of cinematic shark fantasies, evocations of the woman–shark *vagina dentata* have been decidedly negative, serving to eliminate transgressive, non-phallocentric female desire by inspiring primal fears, and perpetuating damaging hierarchies in discourses of heterosexuality (Harrington, 2018; Potts, 2002). Despite these enduring associations, Harrington (drawing on Potts, 2002) argues that the energy and violence inherent in *vagina dentata* can also be reframed and mobilised as an emancipatory force 'through which women can reclaim their bodies, resist corporeal colonisation, or retaliate against a conceptual framing of masculine sexual prowess that serves to denigrate, objectify and subjugate women' (p. 65).

To mobilise my own reimaginings, in the following section I revisit three accounts of human–animal entanglements. These are found in a fairy tale, an insect, and my own excitement of swimming with sharks in the Australian ocean. In these explorations I travel through the discursive and material worlds in which human and non-human animals mingle.

If we accept that *Jaws* is based on the myth of Overcoming the Monster, we might find inspiration for reimagining human relationships with monstrous animals in the revision of classic fairy tales. One rich and useful source is the tale of *Little Red Riding Hood*, the early versions penned by Charles Perrault (1697) and the Grimm brothers (1812), and later retellings through a feminist lens. The Disneyfied version of *Red Riding Hood* that was familiar in my childhood is, when viewed through a feminist lens, a didactic cautionary tale told to children, and especially girls, to police female sexuality and reinforce normative heterosexual hierarchies. The lesson was simple. Women and girls must always beware of the wolf, or in other iterations, the shark; the vulnerable young woman in distress—at risk of seduction by the predatory, lascivious beast—must guard her chastity and await rescue by the worthy male hero.

In the wake of second-wave feminism, some erotic revisions of *Little Red* and similar tales of female-and-beast focus on the young heroine's own wildness: she is no longer a victim but rather a figure of strength and female empowerment, her agency restored (Lau, 2008; Orenstein, 2002, 2004). Although such retellings have become 'essential to the feminist project of dismantling patriarchal understandings of women's sexuality', Lau (2008) suggests that erotic fairy tales risk remaining within dominant male fantasies of the sexualised and sexually available female who abandons reckless adventures and ultimately conforms to heterosexual norms. Seen this way, such revisions prove inadequate to the task of escaping an oppressive patriarchal sexual order (Snowden, 2010).

More intentionally experimental fairy tale retellings offer unsettling transformations and a mixture of danger and desire enfolded into open-ended narratives. In this vein, Angela Carter's celebrated and subversive gothic tale, *The Company of Wolves* (1984), resists dichotomising stereotypes by imagining a more ambiguous human–animal erotic: the girl's metamorphosis into a wolf—the animal projection of female libido—with the heroine embracing her own animal desires in a way that nevertheless 'challenges the traditional negative association of women's sexuality with beastliness' (Snowden, 2010, p. 167). Further beastly confusions are revealed in Kaplan's (1997) short film *Little Red Riding Hood*. In this version, the beast's androgynous sexuality invites a queer reading of the fairy tale, in a move that defies hegemonic, patriarchal gender representations (female victim/male hero) and the bestial Othering of non-human animals inherent in the traditional narrative. Queer retellings may also resist the typical pattern of counter narratives that simply reverse traditional, linguistically embedded binary oppositions—girl/beast, female/male, prey/predator, animal/human, nature/culture—on the basis that these reversals ultimately leave structural binaries intact (Lau, 2008; Orme, 2015). In Kaplan's version of *Little Red Riding Hood*, a curious, capable Little Red is erotically attracted to the sensual, playful, androgynous animal—'both wolf and man and neither' (Orme, 2015, p. 98)—in a joyful, transgressive, and intimate cross-species relationship. By blurring these foundational binaries, queer versions of human–beast stories open up possibilities for seeing our relationship with the wider natural world in different, less fearful and domineering ways.

A release from patriarchal hierarchies might also be inspired by the world of insects, in particular the *Mantis religiosa,* or praying mantis, and the inclination of the female mantis to dismember and devour the male in the act of coitus. In her discussion of 'animal sex', feminist philosopher Elizabeth Grosz (1995) posits that the habits of the female mantis haunt the imaginations and projections of men by representing, through the fantasy of *vagina dentata*, 'an intimate persistent link between sex and death, between pleasure and punishment, desire and revenge' (p. 278). Grosz traces this fear of *vagina dentata* to a Freudian, male-centred model of sexuality that sees male orgasm as the ultimate measure of sexual success and casts female sexuality as voracious, insatiable, and intent on castration of the male. This model has, according to Grosz, constricting effects on female (and male) sexuality because it fails to capture the full potential of desire, passion, and sensuality, which are not reducible to orgasm but have their own thriving, living 'restless impetus' (p. 293). Writing more than 20 years ago, Grosz argued that releasing female sexuality from patriarchal models was 'crucial at this historical conjuncture', and it seems to be just as crucial in the present #metoo era when public attention has been focussed on men's practices of entitlement in the physical and discursive control of women's bodies. In the project of liberation from patriarchal norms, there may still be inspiration to be drawn from the lively habits of our animal and insect cousins, and by imagining the powerful agency of the wolf and the female mantis. For those of us who swim with sharks, perhaps a similar inspiration is possible in the ocean.

Revisiting Jaws *and the Mantis*

I confess that I never saw *Jaws* the movie at the time of its release. In the 1970s I was a pretentious youngster who saw only foreign films and would never have deigned to watch a popular Hollywood blockbuster. Yet in recent years my interest in cultural representations of sharks enticed me to view *Jaws* and recognise its value as a significant repository of shark meanings.

My own understanding of *Jaws* is inflected by both environmental concerns and feminist sensibilities. I recognise the body of the shark as a living animal other, not a metaphor but a concrete presence in my immediate world of ocean swimming. This is another body to be regarded with caution and with respect: I'm wary, I keep my distance, but nevertheless I'm drawn by desire—for beauty, for grace, for wildness. I'm also drawn by curiosity

Figure 6.1 Shark Swishes Away to Freedom
Source: (photo Nick Dawkins)

and the sense of wonder that I will never truly comprehend the shark, or any other animal, 'as any (illusion of) understanding these species requires human discourses which can never capture their essence' (Fuchs, 2015, p. 49). They live their own lives, for the most part, as if we didn't exist: we are of no interest or use, 'negligible, quite frankly, ignored' by these other animals (Wajcman, 2009, p. 128).

The shark, like all animals, cannot be confined to a role in which she is cast as the passive object of scientific research or discursive representation. The agency of the shark, in the real world and in movies, continues to disrupt 'the smooth unfolding of Enlightenment ideology' as she resists the imperialist desire to map, decode, and represent the entire natural world from the human point of view (Armstrong, 2002, p. 415). In the face of the powerful shark, humans can be emptied of their self-proclaimed specialness as the centre of the universe, reduced to their material dimension, rendered available as an object of predation in a world where we are all food. This perspective, proposed so strongly by environmentalist Val Plumwood (2012) following her experience of being attacked by a crocodile, helps us to see ourselves in ecological terms as part of a much larger interwoven web of matter and flesh.

In closing, and drawing inspiration from the female mantis, I choose to read an energising sense of libidinous agency in the shark as totem for female power. In the same way that feminist retellings of *Little Red Riding Hood* focus on her empowerment and playfulness, either in defeating the wolf, in becoming the wolf, in actively seducing him, or in simply walking away from his predatory gaze, I identify with the shark, her independence, her agency, and her slippery elusiveness. Confounding taxonomic boundaries, resisting coercive representation, refusing hyperfeminine identity, post-animal pre-human, prehistoric posthistory, native alien, unknowable, obscure, incomprehensible, whimsical, indefinable, becoming-animal, I desire affinity with the shark. Implacably Other. No arms, no legs, no pussy to grab, no breasts to ogle: with the shark, all you see is muscle and fluid movement. She doesn't respond to your needs and desires, she ignores you, she'd rather swim away. Unruly, uncontrollable, unpredictable, she avoids interference, except on her own terms. If threatened with patriarchal provocations, she threatens revenge in return. If you invade her space she might bite you, maim you. The shark has perfect teeth. At times, as a woman, I would like to be a shark or ray, sovereign animals of such absolute beauty who swim by and simply ignore us, the spectators, indifferent to our desires, interests, and intentions. In her indifference 'there's a kind of lover's scorn in play' (Wajcman, 2009, p. 134) as she swishes away to freedom.

Notes

1. Jaws (1975) Quint is devoured by the shark, movie clip. Available at: www.youtube.com/watch?v=pmLP0QQPqFw&t=0s&list=PLZbXA4lyCtqrbRxPpGT tJmuKFumWfw7l3&index=10
2. Jaws (1975) Brody kills the shark, movie clip. Available at: www.youtube.com/watch?v=FpxOLhuNXfM&t=0s&list=PLZbXA4lyCtqrbRxPpGTtJmuKFumW fw7l3&index=11
3. See, for example, movie posters for *The Shallows*. Available at: https://en.wikipedia.org/wiki/The_Shallows_(film); for *Shark Night*. Available at: https://en.wikipedia.org/wiki/Shark_Night; and for *Deep Blue Sea*. Available at: https://en.wikipedia.org/wiki/Deep_Blue_Sea_(1999_film)

7 Afterword

In order to face the large-scale, complex problems of environmental degradation, mass extinctions, and climate change, we first need smaller stories and encounters that engage with human affect, curiosity, imagination, and reason. These stories can also respond to calls for multimodal language studies scholars to engage ecologically, and for new types of language and writing adequate for post-anthropocentrism: 'the resources of the imagination, as well as the tools of critical intelligence, need to be enlisted for the task' (Braidotti, 2013, p. 82).

In this series of essays I've offered some small stories to explore various aspects of human–shark relationships through a feminist lens. Focussing on these two entangled animals—the *shark* and the *human*—has been a way of entering into two contemporary conversations: first, about human relationships with a more-than-human world in a living planet; and second, about continuing concerns around the oppressive effects of normative heterosexuality and hegemonic masculinity. Each chapter has presented a collection of images, events, material bodies (of people and other species), emotions, discourses, texts, apparatuses, ideas, phenomena, memories, objects, locations and times, brought together as 'potentially useful assemblages for ongoing learning' (Toohey, 2018, p. 7). At times these assemblages are seen to produce or reflect fixed, destructive ways of experiencing or enacting the intersections of humans, sharks, and gender relationships. At other times, there's a scent of freedom.

In closing, I want to consider some personal accounts of human–shark relationships that emerge from my own energising, embodied experiences of swimming in the ocean. The first recollections reflect on the consequences of our disregard for the natural world. The others point to more open ways of thinking and seeing the world differently. Together, these stories can be seen as another form of entangled pedagogy, an alternative to hegemonic masculinity, and a playful engagement with shape-shifting assemblages of bodies, images, phenomena, and language that celebrate opportunities for a joyous, embodied learning with sharks.

The readers I address here are those who seek an always-new relationship with the more-than-human world, those who are 'multiply entangled and who yearn to more fully engage with the world, rather than remove themselves from it' (Toohey, 2018, p. 6).

Swimming and Mourning With Sharks

06:00 Shelly Beach, NSW coast: Late summer and the air and water are warm. I slip into the salty ocean as an assemblage of body, lycra and plastic goggles, hoping to swim with sharks. My feet leave the sandy bottom and I look straight down as I glide over waving seaweeds and schools of tiny fish. When I meet a massive school of yellowtail I reach out in the vain attempt to touch their shiny bodies with mine. I know I never will, they dart away so quickly. I keep swimming steadily, breathing from side to side, heading towards the area that my swim friends call 'shark alley'. Then I see one, two, a dozen or more: dusky whaler sharks. Their muscular bodies move through the water so effortlessly, propelled by a graceful tail wave. We have so many with us this season, I'm not sure why. We're grateful for their presence. Later today, a few beaches to the north of where I swim, the bloody bodies of two juvenile dusky whaler sharks are found abandoned on the beach. They each measure only a metre in length, they have hooks in their mouths and their flesh is punctured by stab wounds. Although they've been caught by fishers using hooks and lines, they've not been treasured as food for humans. Rather, it seems, they are trophies. A report of the incident in our local newspaper (Cross, 2016) says the sharks were probably killed for a 'selfie'. How very twenty-first century.

07:00 Shelly Beach, NSW. Winter. This morning the sea is rough and cold. I swim hard to get past the big breakers crashing into the beach, taking a breather in the choppy mess out from the point. Struggle to make the swim to Shelly, so ungainly. Not much to see, visibility poor. I decide to walk back to Manly from Shelly, along Marine Parade, below the houses built into the cliff. I catch up to a friend who's holding aloft a single red gum boot. I laugh in anticipation of some silly antic. Sarah's always funny. But then, embarrassed, I see what the boot is holding, and the look of distress on Sarah's face. It's a shark, its head stuck so far into the maw of the boot that it can't escape. Poor creature, trapped in human waste. This is one individual subject of a life, one among millions killed by careless, profligate, or greedy humans every minute of every day. How have we come to this? I mourn for this single life.

Figure 7.1 Blind Shark Stuck in Red Boot
Source: (photo Elaine de Jager)

Doing Things Differently

Entanglement in the more-than-human world offers an invitation to won-der, to learn, and to think and do things differently. My own journey of swimming with sharks for six years has opened up a new world, stretched my boundaries of curiosity and care, and allowed me to consider how we/I came to think about sharks in certain ways, through the training of cultural heritage. Now we/I think and do differently, there has been a shift for sharks. So many different ways are open, but here I point to some few of my favourites. These are small stories about doing and thinking differently.

One of my fellow swimmers is Mauricio, a very quiet man, one of the quietest I know. He and I share an interest in sharks and in developing the potential for positive and mutually enriching human–animal relationships. He is a free diver. Free divers eschew the bulky equipment of the scuba diver. They dive with no more than a held breath, staying underwater for many magical minutes at a time. Mauricio is also an extraordinary underwa-ter photographer and through his images I see the world differently. Here is Mauricio's *Eye of the Port Jackson shark* (my title, in homage to Val Plum-wood's *Eye of the Crocodile*, 2012), and an extract from our text exchange about entanglement in the more-than-human world.

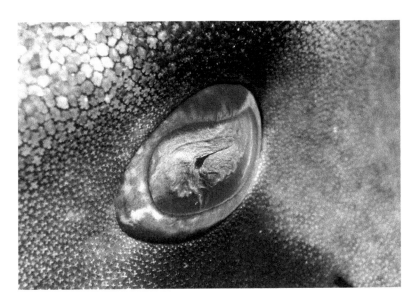

Figure 7.2 Eye of the Port Jackson Shark
Source: (photo Mauricio Fuentes)

MAURICIO: There is a common ground here I can see, I came up with the *projeto contato* idea because I wanted to investigate human-marine animals relationships long time ago, I wanted to know if we can actually connect and contact these animals on their terms and what sort of exchange can happen. I was 21 then, only now living by the sea and having the bay so close I managed to put it to practice and it has been incredible as I realised that yes it is possible to establish a connection based on trust and by presenting ourselves not as a threat, I was very surprised to realise how tolerant and sometimes receptive the animals can be. Which proves how sensorial they are in understanding our behaviour as well. [I've had experiences that] showed me how sensitive [sharks] can be and raised other questions such as how conscious they are of our intentions when recognising and perhaps accepting/enjoying our contact.

I don't see ourselves as superior as we assume we are, there is a lot to be learnt from them and getting closer and understanding, not mentally or rationally but sensorially, opens an interesting perspective on how our relationship with them can evolve.

Figure 7.3 Wobbegong With Plastic Noose
Source: (photo Elaine De Jager)

Figure 7.4 Releasing the Noose
Source: (photo Elaine De Jager)

Figure 7.5 Wobbegong Released
Source: (photo Elaine De Jager)

In our usual swimming location we occasionally see fish and sharks with human waste stuck to them; the sight of fish hooks or tangled plastics in mouths and gills is distressingly common. Because fish and sharks are generally shy of humans (for good reason) it's not often possible to remove the ugly bits of metal and plastic from their bodies. Unless you're like Mauricio, who, I think, is part fish, perhaps a merman.

Mauricio shows me photos of some close experiences with sharks that are both daunting (sharks—and humans—can and do bite) and exceptional in their sensitivity. The photos show a very particular kind of male embodiment: a gentleness and exquisite care borne of curiosity, questioning, and respect. These are creatures who seem to be learning, with patience, from each other.

Imagining Freedom

One of the resources of the imagination available to me has its origin in my Celtic ancestral heritage, in stories told by my grandparents about shape-shifting beings that belong in the seas around Scotland. These fey shape-shifters are selkies, seal creatures who, when on the shore, can shed their skins and take on the appearance of human beings.

Dressing again in their natural skins enables the selkies to return to their watery origins. The selkie stories, with their blurring of multiple boundaries, blend accounts of the human condition with an acute awareness of our kinship with other animals and of our entanglement in the natural world, in this case, the world of the ocean.

In the most frequently told story, a female selkie comes ashore and has her sealskin stolen by a man who, in an act of staggering entitlement, compels her to become his wife. By stealing and hiding her skin, the man robs the selkie woman of her agency and gains control over every aspect of her life. The selkie longs to return to her ocean home. Eventually, after many long years of dutiful marriage, the selkie woman finds and retrieves her sealskin and escapes to the sea, leaving her husband and children behind. In this story, the mythic sealskin is a locus where the supernatural, the irrational, the female, and the animal are intertwined and overlayed (Le Couteur, 2015).

The narrative archetype of the selkie wife speaks to the iniquities of gender and sexuality that inhere in traditional heteronormative codes of marriage, and illuminates the suffering of the selkie woman who is compelled by trickery into performing a feminine role in a patriarchal society. But the story also holds the hope of female sexual and personal empowerment, agency, and freedom, the promise of resistance against assimilation, together with an incitement to engage more fully with the natural world. This is the offer of 'an escape into a less ordered universe where neither the laws of time and space nor the ordinary societal roles and more apply' (Heddle, 2016, p. 3).

With this imaginative inspiration, I picture the swimmer in a shark-shaped denticled skin, a woman/shark hybrid in a liminal space that traverses both ocean and land. The queer shape-shifting shark craves independence from the coercive control exercised by humans over the natural world, and from the patriarchal politics of gender. Ever subversive and unruly, she resists assimilation or colonising domestication. She is an embodied and political inspiration in a time of feminist resurgence. Her story is the story of the future.

References

Afonso, A.S., Cantareli, C.V., Levy, R.P. & Veras, L.B. (2016). Evasive mating behaviour by female nurse sharks. *Ginglymostoma cirratum* (Bonnaterre, 1788), in an equatorial insular breeding ground. *Neotropical Ichthyology*, *14*(4). doi:10.1590/1982-0224-20160103

Ahlberg, P.E. (2009). Birth of the jawed vertebrates. *Nature*, *457*, 1094–1095.

Ahlberg, P.E., Trinajstik, K., Johanson, Z. & Long, J. (2009). Pelvic claspers confirm chondrichthyan-like internal fertilization in arthrodires. *Nature*, *460*, 888–889. doi:10.1038/nature08176

Allam, L. (2015). Indigenous cultural views of the shark. *Earshot*. ABC Radio National Transcripts. Retrieved from www.abc.net.au/radionational/programs/earshot/indigenous-cultural-views-of-the-shark/6798174

Aloi, G. (2011). *Art and animals*. London and New York: I.B. Taurus.

Andrzejaczek, S., Meeuwig, J., Rowat, D., Pierce, S., Davies, T., Fisher, R. & Meekam, M. (2016). The ecological connectivity of whale shark aggregations in the Indian Ocean: A photo-identification. *Royal Society Open Science*, *3*(11), 160455. http://dx.doi.org/10.1098/rsos.160455

Appleby, R. (2012). Dog days. In H. Weisert & E.A. Stone (Eds.), *Animal companions, animal doctors, animal people* (pp. 110–111). Ontario: Ontario Veterinary College, University of Guelph.

Appleby, R. (2015). Julia Gillard: A murderous rage. In J. Wilson & D. Boxer (Eds.), *Discourse, politics, and women as global leaders*, pp. 149–167. Amsterdam: John Benjamins.

Appleby, R. & Pennycook, A. (2017). Swimming with sharks, ecological feminism and posthuman language politics. *Critical Inquiry in Language Studies*, *14*(2–3), 239–261. doi: 10.1080/15427587.2017.1279545

Ardern, L. & Wurth, R. (2014, May 28). Bianca bears the scars. *Gold Coast Bulletin*, p. 4.

Armstrong, P. (2002). The postcolonial animal. *Society & Animals*, *10*(4), 413–419.

Ashcroft, B. (2013). Hybridity and transformation: The art of Lin Onus. *Postcolonial Text*, *8*(1), 1–18.

Ashton, K. (2009). *John Singleton Copley's Watson and the shark: A collaborative representation of Brook Watson* (Unpublished MA thesis). Lehigh University, Bethlehem, PA.

Atwood, T.B, Connolly, R.M., Ritchie, E.G., Lovelock, C.E., Heithaus, M.R., Hays, G.C., Fourqurean, J.W. & Macreadie, P.I. (2015). Predators help protect carbon stocks in blue carbon ecosystems. *Nature Climate Change, 5*, 1038–1045.

Australian Marine Conservation Society (ACMS) (2017). *Shark finning*. Retrieved from www.marineconservation.org.au/pages/shark-finning.html

Baker, S. (1993). *Picturing the beast: Animals, identity and representation*. Manchester: Manchester University Press.

Baker, S. (2000). *The postmodern animal*. London: Reaktion Books.

Baker, S. (2013). *Artist | animal*. Minneapolis: University of Minnesota Press.

Banks, L. (2015, August 6). Great white shark survivor promises: I'm never going in the sea again. *Daily Telegraph*, p. 3.

Barad, K. (2007). *Meeting the universe halfway: Quantum physics and the entanglement of matter and meaning*. Durham, NC and London: Duke University Press.

Barthes, R. (1982). *Camera lucida: Reflections on photography*. New York, NY: Hill and Wang.

Bennett, J. (2010). A vitalist stopover on the way to a new materialism. In D. Coole & S. Frost (Eds.), *New materialisms: Ontology, agency and politics*. Durham, NC: Duke University Press.

Berger, J. (1972). *Ways of seeing*. London: Penguin.

Bernal, M.A., Sinai, N.L., Rocha, C., Gaither, M.R., Dunker, F. & Rocha, L.A. (2015). Long-term sperm storage in the brownbanded bamboo shark *Chiloscyllium punctatum*. *Journal of Fish Biology, 86*, 1171–1176.

Birke, L. (2002). Intimate familiarities? Feminism and human–animal studies. *Society and Animals, 10*(4), 429–436.

Bishop, J. (2013). Ken Thaiday senior, Darnley man. *Artlink, 33*(2), 77–79.

Biskind, P. (1975). *Jaws*: Between the teeth. *Jump Cut: A Review of Contemporary Media, 9*. Retrieved from www.ejumpcut.org/archive/onlinessays/JC09folder/Jaws.html

Boime, A. (1989). Blacks in shark-infested waters: Visual encodings of racism in Copley and Homer. *Smithsonian Studies in American Art, 3*(1), 18–47.

Boissonneault, M.F., Gladstone, W., Scott, P. & Cushing, N. (2005). Grey nurse shark human interactions and portrayals: A study of newspaper portrayals of the grey nurse shark from 1969–2003. *Electronic Green Journal, 1*(22). Retrieved from https://escholarship.org/uc/item/9nb9h48n

Bonfil, R., Meÿer, M., Scholl, M.C., Johnson, R., O'Brien, S., Oosthuizen, H., . . . Paterson, M. (2005, October 10). Transoceanic migration, spatial dynamics, and population linkages of white sharks. *Science, 310*, 100–103.

Booker, C. (2004). *The seven basic plots: Why we tell stories*. London: Continuum.

Booth, D. (2001). From bikinis to boardshorts: Wahines and the paradoxes of surfing culture. *Journal of Sport History, 28*(1), 3–22.

Bowles, S.E. (1976). The exorcist and Jaws. *Literature/Film Quarterly, 4*(3), 196–214.

Braidotti, R. (2013). *The posthuman*. Cambridge: Polity.

Briggs, C. (2017, January 17). Townsville aquarium's leopard shark switches to asexual reproduction in extreme form of inbreeding. *ABC News*. Retrieved from www.abc.net.au/news/2017-01-16/townsville-leopard-sharks-switches-asexual-reproduction/8186126

Broglio, R. (2008). 'Living flesh': Animal-human surfaces. *Journal of Visual Culture*, *7*(1), 103–121.

Broglio, R. (2011). *Surface encounters: Thinking with animals and art*. Minneapolis: University of Minnesota Press.

Brown, E. (2016). How a century of fear turned deadly for sharks. *Florida Museum*. Retrieved from www.floridamuseum.ufl.edu/science/how-a-century-of-fear-turned-deadly-for-sharks/

Bryson, B. (2000). *Down under: Travels in a sunburned country*. London: Doubleday.

Burgess, G. (2015, July 22). White shark populations are growing: Here's why that's good news. *The Conversation*. Retrieved from https://theconversation.com/white-shark-populations-are-growing-heres-why-thats-good-news-44872

Bush, L. (2016). Creating our own lineup: Identities and shared cultural norms of surfing women in a U.S. east coast community. *Journal of Contemporary Ethnography*, *45*(3), 290–318.

Byrne, R.J. & Avise, J.C. (2012). Genetic mating system of the brown smoothhound shark (*Mustelus henlei*), including a literature review of multiple paternity in other elasmobranch species. *Marine Biology*, *159*, 749–756.

Calarco, M. (2015). *Thinking through animals: Identity, difference and indistinction*. Stanford, CA: Stanford Briefs.

Callinan, R. (2009, January 12). Sharks rampage in Australia. *Time Magazine*. Retrieved from http://content.time.com/time/world/article/0,8599,1871007,00.html

Cameron, D. (2016, August 22). *Familiarity and contempt*. Retrieved from https://debuk.wordpress.com/2016/08/22/familiarity-and-contempt

Cameron, D. (2017, December 28). 2017: *The year in language and feminism*. Retrieved from https://debuk.wordpress.com/2017/12/28/2017-the-year-in-language-and-feminism/

Caputi, J. (1978). *Jaws* as patriarchal myth. *Journal of Popular Film*, *6*, 305–326.

Carroll, M.D. (1989). The erotics of absolutism: Rubens and the mystification of sexual violence. *Representations*, *25*, 3–30.

Caruana, W. (2012). *Aboriginal art* (3rd ed.). London: Thames & Hudson.

Castro, J.I. (2002). On the origins of the Spanish word 'tibur´on', and the English word 'shark'. *Environmental Biology of Fishes*, *65*, 249–253.

Chambers, G. & Lion, P. (2014, April 4). Husband saw maneater. *The Daily Telegraph*, p. 2.

Chapman, D.D., Prodöhl, D.A., Gelsleichter, J., Manire, C.A. & Shivji, M.S. (2004). Predominance of genetic monogamy by females in a hammerhead shark, *Sphyrna tiburo*: Implications for shark conservation. *Molecular Ecology*, *13*, 1965–1974. doi:10.1111/j.1365-294X.2004.02178.x

Chapman, D.D., Shivji, M.S., Louis, E., Sommer, J., Fletcher, H. & Prodöhl, D.A. (2007). Virgin birth in a hammerhead shark. *Biology Letters*, *3*, 425–427.

Chenery (2005, October 3). Global shark experts meet in Sydney to discuss rising attacks. *The Saturday Paper*. Retrieved from www.thesaturdaypaper.com.au/news/environment/2015/10/03/global-shark-experts-meet-sydney-discuss-rising-attacks/14437944002457

Chernov, J. & Ripetungi (2013). *Shark attack*. Retrieved from http://ripetungi.com/wp-content/uploads/Shark-Attack-Stop-Finning-Infographic.png

Choi, C.Q. (2010, June 20). How 'Jaws' forever changed our view of great white sharks. *Live Science*. Retrieved from www.livescience.com/8309-jaws-changed-view-great-white-sharks.html

Choi, C.Q. (2012, January 8). 'Virgin birth' record broken by hotel shark. *National Geographic*. Retrieved from https://news.nationalgeographic.com/news/2012/01/120106-virgin-birth-shark-dubai-science/

Chris, C. (2006). *Watching wildlife*. Minneapolis: University of Minnesota Press.

Clancy, J. (2012). Human agency and the myth of divine salvation in Copley's *Watson and the shark*. *American Art, 26*(1), 102–111.

Clarke, S.C., McAllister, M.K., Milner-Gulland, E.J., Kirkwood, G.P., Michielsens, C.G.J., Agnew, D.J., . . . Shivji, M.H. (2006). Global estimates of shark catches using trade records from commercial markets. *Ecology Letters, 9*, 1115–1126.

Cook, G. (2015). 'A pig is a person' or 'You can love a fox and hunt it': Innovation and tradition in the discursive representation of animals. *Discourse & Society, 26*, 587–607.

Costa, D.P., Breed, G.A. & Robinson, P.W. (2012). New insights into pelagic migrations: Implications for conservation and management. *Annual Review of Ecology, Environment and Systematics, 43*, 73–96.

Coward, R. (1984). *Female desire*. London: Paladin.

Cox, P. (2015). *Violence against women in Australia: Additional analysis of the Australian Bureau of Statistics' Personal Safety Survey, 2012*. Sydney: ANROWS.

Crabb, A. (2006, July 2). The shark hunter, the artist, and a nice little earner. *The Age*. Retrieved from www.theage.com.au/news/national/the-shark-hunter-the-artist-and-a-nice-little-earner/2006/07/01/1151174441325.html

Crawford, D. (2008). *Shark*. London: Reaktion Books.

Creed, B. (1993). *Phallic panic: Film, horror and the primal uncanny*. Melbourne: Melbourne University Press.

Crosby, C. (2017). Can social media give sharks a better reputation? *Smithsonian Magazine*. Retrieved from www.smithsonianmag.com/innovation/can-social-media-give-sharks-better-reputation-180962411/

Cross, J. (2016, February 26). Dusky whaler sharks may have been 'knifed' and killed for a selfie. *Daily Telegraph*. Retrieved from http://www.dailytelegraph.com.au/newslocal/northern-beaches/dusky-whaler-sharks-may-have-beenknifed-and-killed-for-a-selfie/news-story/e2241cdae5c177dad3815544f964a631

Crowther, B. (1995). Towards a feminist critique of television natural history programmes. In P. Florence & D. Reynolds (Eds.), *Feminist subjects, Multi-media: Cultural methodologies* (pp. 127–146). Manchester: Manchester University Press.

Crowther, B. (1999). The birds and the bees: Narratives of sexuality in television natural history programmes. In D. Epstein & J.T. Sears (Eds.), *A dangerous knowing: Sexuality, pedagogy and popular culture* (pp. 43–58). London: Continuum.

Crowther, B. & Leith, D. (1995). Feminism, language and the rhetoric of television wildlife programmes. In S. Mills (Ed.), *Language and gender: Interdisciplinary perspectives* (pp. 207–225). Londong and New York: Longman.

Dapin, M. (2016, February 6). Shark attack survivors bite back. *Sydney Morning Herald*. Retrieved from www.smh.com.au/good-weekend/shark-attack-survivors-bite-back-20160202-gmk7jv.html

de Beauvoir, S. (1972). *The second sex*. Trans. H.M. Parshley. New York: Vintage.

Dennis, C. (2008, May 29). The oldest pregnant mum. *Nature*, *453*, 575. doi:10.1038/453575a

Derrida, J. (2008). *The animal that therefore I am*. M.L. Mallet, Ed. and D. Wills, Trans. New York: Fordham University Press.

DiChristina, M. (2011). Casting a wide net. *Scientific American*, *304*, 8.

Domeier, M.L. & Nasby-Lucas, N. (2013). Two-year migration of adult female white sharks (*Carcharodon carcharias*) reveals widely separated nursery areas and conservation concerns. *Animal Biotelemetry*, *1*, 2. doi:10.1186/2050-3385-1-2

Drummond, L. (1996). *American dreamtime: A cultural analysis of popular movies and their implications for a science of humanity*. Lanham, MD: Littlefield Adams.

Dudgeon, C.L., Coulton, L., Bone, R., Ovenden, J.R. & Thomas, S. (2017). Switch from sexual to parthenogenetic reproduction in a zebra shark. *Scientific Reports*, *7*(40537), 1–6. doi:10.1038/srep40537

Easteal, P., Holland, K. & Judd, K. (2015). Enduring themes and silences in media portrayals of violence against women. *Women's Studies International Forum 28*, 103–113.

Eather, M. (2000). 'Under the influence': The collaborative world of Lin Onus. In M. Neale (Ed.), *Urban dingo: The art and life of Lin Onus 1948–1996* (pp. 55–59). Brisbane: Queensland Art Gallery.

Ebert, R. (2016). *The shallows*. Retrieved from www.rogerebert.com/reviews/the-shallows-2016

Eccles, J. (2017, May 28). Red Ochre for Ken Thaiday. *Aboriginal Art Directory*. Retrieved from https://news.aboriginalartdirectory.com/2017/05/red-ochre-for-ken-thaiday.php

Eilperin, J. (2011). *Demon fish: Travels through the hidden world of sharks*. New York: Pantheon Book.

Elbra, J. (2012, August 13). Australia not doing enough to prevent shark finning. *The Conversation*. Retrieved from https://theconversation.com/australia-not-doing-enough-to-prevent-shark-finning-8765

Evans, V. (2014). *The language myth: Why language is not an instinct*. Cambridge: Cambridge University Press.

Feldheim, K.A., Chapman, D.D., Sweet, D., Fitzpatrick, S., Prodöhl, D.A., Shivji, M.S. & Snowdon, B. (2010). Shark virgin birth produces multiple, viable offspring. *Journal of Heredity*, *101*(3), 374–377.

Fields, A.T., Fischer, G.A., Shea, S.K.H., Zhang, H., Abercrombie D.L, Feldheim, K.A., Babcock, E.A. & Chapman, D.D. (2017). Species composition of the international shark fin trade assessed through a retail-market survey in Hong Kong. *Conservation Biology*, *32*(2), 376–389.

Fitzpatrick, J.L., Kempster, R.M., Daly-Engel, T.S., Collin, S.P. & Evans, J.P. (2012). Assessing the potential for post-copulatory sexual selection in elasmobranchs. *Journal of Fish Biology*, *80*, 1141–1158. doi:10.1111/j.1095-8649.2012.03256.x

Fluffy the great white shark heads back to sea. (2017, September 12). *Daily Mail*. Retrieved from www.dailymail.co.uk/wires/afp/article-4875268/Fluffy-great-white-shark-heads-sea.html

Foley, M. (2000). Forward. In M. Neale (Ed.), *Urban dingo: The art and life of Lin Onus 1948–1996* (p. 8). Brisbane: Queensland Art Gallery.

Fraiman, S. (2012). Pussy panic versus liking animals: Tracking gender in animal studies. *Critical Inquiry, 39*, 89–115.

Francis, B. (2011). Before and after *Jaws*: Changing representations of shark attacks. *Great Circle, 34*(2), 44–64.

Fuchs, M. (2015). 'They are a fact of life out here': The ecocritical subtexts of three early-twenty-first-century Aussie animal horror movies. In K. Gregersdotter, J. Höglund & N. Hållén (Eds.), *Animal horror movies: Genre, history and criticism* (pp. 37–57). Basingstoke, UK: Palgrave Macmillan.

Gaard, G. (2011). Ecofeminism revisited: Rejecting essentialism and re-placing species in a material feminist environmentalism. *Feminist Formations, 23*(2), 26–53.

Garlick, S. (2017). The return of nature: Feminism, hegemonic masculinities, and new materialisms. *Men and Masculinities*. doi.org/10.1177/1097184X17725128

Gibbs, L. (2015, July 20). Spectacular shark encounters: Fanning's close shave reminds us we share the ocean. *The Conversation*. Retrieved from https://theconversation.com/spectacular-shark-encounters-fannings-close-shave-reminds-us-we-share-the-ocean-44910

Gibbs, L. & Warren, A. (2015). Transforming shark hazard policy: Learning from ocean-users and shark encounter in Western Australia. *Marine Policy, 58*, 116–124. http://dx.doi.org/10.1016/j.marpol.2015.04.014

Giordiani, A. (2013, April 10). Female great whites reveal long range mating secrets. *New Scientist*. Retrieved from www.newscientist.com/article/dn23364-female-great-whites-reveal-long-range-mating-secrets/

Giroux, H. (2008). Hollywood film as public pedagogy: Education in the crossfire. *Afterimage, 35*(5), 7–13.

Global Shark Attack File (n.d.). *GSAF incident log by country*. Retrieved from http://sharkattackfile.net/incidentlog.htm

Godfrey, M. (2015, September 2). Net gain for sanity. *The Daily Telegraph*, p. 4.

Graves, R. (1961). *The white goddess: A historical grammar of poetic myth*. London: Faber & Faber.

Gregersdotter, K., Höglund, J. & Hållén, N. (Eds.). (2015). *Animal horror cinema: Genre, history and criticism*. London: Palgrave Macmillan.

Grosz, E. (1995). Animal sex. In E. Grosz & E. Probyn (Eds.), *Sexy bodies: The strange carnalities of feminism* (pp. 278–299). London and New York: Routledge.

Gruen, L. (1993). Dismantling oppression: an analysis of the connection between women and animals. In G. Gaard (Ed.), *Ecofeminism: Women, animals, nature* (pp. 60–90). Philadelphia, PA: Temple University Press.

Gruen, L. & Weil, K. (2010). Teaching difference: Sex, gender, species. In M. De Mello (Ed.), *Teaching the animal* (pp. 127–142). Brooklyn: Lantern.

Gruen, L. & Weil, K. (2012). Animal others: Editors' introduction. *Hypatia, 27*(3), 477–487. http://dx.doi.org/10.1111/j.1527-2001.2012.01296.x

Hammerschlag, N., Gallagher, A.J. & Lazarre, D.M. (2011). A review of shark satellite tagging studies. *Journal of Experimental Marine Biology and Ecology*, *398*, 1–8.

Hamscha, S. (2013). *The fiction of America: Performance and the cultural imaginary in literature and film*. Frankfurt: Campus Verlag.

Haraway, D. (1978). Animal sociology and a natural economy of the body politic, Part II: The past is the contested zone: Human nature and theories of production and reproduction in primate behavior studies. *Signs: Journal of Women in Culture and Society*, *4*(1), 37–60.

Haraway, D. (2003). *The companion species manifesto: Dogs, people, and significant otherness*. Chicago: Prickly Paradigm.

Haraway, D. (2008). *When species meet*. Minneapolis: University of Minnesota Press.

Harrington, E. (2018). *Women, monstrosity and horror film: Gynaehorror*. London and New York: Routledge.

Harris, A. (2013). Financial artscapes: Damien Hirst, crisis and the city of London. *Cities*, *33*, 29–35.

Heddle, D. (2016, December). Selkies, sex, and the supernatural. *The Bottle Imp*, *20*, p. 1–3.

Hinds, R. (2015, July 26). Bravery's greatest hits. *The Daily Telegraph*, p. 92.

Hoskins, I. (2014). *The shift for sharks*. Retrieved from http://ianhoskins.com

Howard, B.C. (2013, June 7). Record-breaking Mako shark tips off conservation debate. *National Geographic*. Retrieved from https://news.nationalgeographic.com/news/2013/06/130606-record-mako-shark-california-conservation/

Irving, M. (2017, January 18). Lonely leopard shark learns to reproduce herself. *New Atlas*. Retrieved from https://newatlas.com/endangered-zebra-shark-switches-sexual-asexual-reproduction/47427/

Jaffe, I.B. (1977). John Singleton Copley's *Watson and the shark*. *American Art Journal*, *9*, 15–25.

Jameson, F. (1979). Reification and utopia in mass culture. *Social Text*, *1*, 130–148.

Jorgensen, S.J., Arnoldi, N.S., Estess, E.E., Chapple, T.K., Rückert, M., Anderson, S.D. & Block, B.A. (2012). Eating or mating? Cluster analysis reveals intricacies of white shark (*Carcharodon carcharias*) migration and offshore behavior. *PLos One*, *7*(10), e47819. doi:10.1371/journal.pone.0047819

Jorgensen, S.J., Reeb, C.A., Chapple, T.K., Anderson, S., Perle, C., Van Sommeran, S.R., . . . Block, B.A. (2010). Philopatry and migration of Pacific white sharks. *Proceedings of the Royal Society B*, *277*, 679–688.

Kaplan, D. (Director) (1997). *Little Red Riding Hood* [DVD recording]. Retrieved from www.youtube.com/watch?v=sHUvdG-fCx0

Kay, B. (2017). Incredible twist to tail. *Manly Daily*, p. 1, 5. Retrieved from http://newslocal.smedia.com.au/manly-daily/

Kay, B. & Lowe, A. (2017, September 12). Shark washes up at Manly. *Manly Daily*, p. 1, 11. Retrieved from http://newslocal.smedia.com.au/manly-daily/

Keene, N. (2015, July 25). Jaws of death stalk shores. *The Daily Telegraph*, p. 59.

King, R. (2014, March). For the love of sharks. *The Monthly*, pp. 20–25.

Klein, A. (2017, January 16). Female shark learns to reproduce without males after years along. *New Scientist*. Retrieved from www.newscientist.com/article/2118052-female-shark-learns-to-reproduce-without-males-after-years-alone/

Knox, M. (2015, July 20). Mick Fanning shark attack one of the most surreal near-death experiences seen on live TV. *The Sydney Morning Herald*. Retrieved from www.smh.com.au

Kretzmann, S. (2012, April 23). Fatal shark attack leads to condemnation of shark adventure filming adventure. *West Cape News*. Retrieved from http://westcapenews.com/?p=4112

Laing, A. (2015, July 20). 'Small' great white shark did not intend to kill surfer Mick Fanning, say experts. *The Telegraph UK*. Retrieved from www.telegraph.co.uk/news/worldnews

Landers, R. (2017). *Hooked on: Katherine the shark* [Video file]. Retrieved from www.facebook.com/SharkLand/videos/786670681535330/

Laschon, E. (2017). WA shark attack: Western Australia rejects call for cull after fatal mauling near Esperance. *ABC News*. Retrieved from www.abc.net.au/news/2017-04-19/wa-shark-attack-esperance-australia-cull-laeticia-brouwer/8453468

Latour, B. (1993). *We have never been modern*. (C. Porter, Trans.). Cambridge, MA: Harvard University Press.

Lau, K.J. (2008). Erotic infidelities: Angela Carter's wolf trilogy. *Marvels & Tales: Journal of Fairy-Tale Studies*, *22*(1), 77–94.

Lawrence, D. & Lawrence, H.R. (2004). Torres Strait: The region and its people. In R. Davis (Ed.), *Woven histories, dancing lives: Torres Strait Islander identity, culture and history* (pp. 15–29). Canberra: Aboriginal Studies Press.

Leber, J. (2018, July 23). What's it like to personify a shark on Twitter. *News Deeply*. Retrieved from www.newsdeeply.com/oceans/community/2018/07/23/what-its-like-to-personify-a-shark-on-twitter

Le Couteur, P. (2015). Slipping off the sealskin: Gender, species, and fictive kinship in selkie folktales. *Gender Forum*, *55*, 55–82.

Lee, J.J. (2014, March 13). Scientists track a great white shark across the Atlantic for the first time. *National Geographic*. Retrieved from https://news.nationalgeographic.com/news/2014/03/140311-great-white-shark-atlantic-ocean-crossing-animal-science/

Leigo, T. & Adcock, F. (2016, February 1). Vic Hislop's Shark Show closes doors after 30 years in Hervey Bay. *ABC News*. Retrieved from www.abc.net.au/news/2016-02-01/vic-hislop-shark-show-closes-hervey-bay/7129802

Little, B. (2017, January 18). Shark surprises aquarium with rare 'virgin birth'. *National Geographic*. Retrieved from https://news.nationalgeographic.com/2017/01/zebra-shark-virgin-birth-reproduction/

Long, J.A. (2011, January). Dawn of the deed. *Scientific American*, *304*, 34–39. doi:10.1038/scientificamerican0111-34

Long, J.A. (2014, October 20). Copulate to populate: Ancient Scottish fish did it sideways. *The Conversation*. Retrieved from https://theconversation.com/copulate-to-populate-ancient-scottish-fish-did-it-sideways-30910

Long, J.A., Mark-Kurik, E., Johanson, Z., Lee, M.S.Y., Young, G.C., Min, Z., . . . Trinajstic, K. (2015). Copulation in antiarch placoderms and the origin of gnathostome internal fertilization. *Nature*, *517*, 196–199.

Long, J.A. & Trinajstic, K. (2014, June 9). The first vertebrate sexual organs evolved as an extra pair of legs. *The Conversation*. Retrieved from https://theconversation.com/the-first-vertebrate-sexual-organs-evolved-as-an-extra-pair-of-legs-27578

Long, J.A., Trinajstic, K. & Johanson, Z. (2009, February 26). Devonian arthrodires embryos and the origin of internal fertilization in vertebrates. *Nature, 457*, 1124–1127. doi:10.1038/nature07732

Long, J.A., Trinajstic, K., Young, G.C. & Sneden, T. (2008). Live birth in the Devonian period. *Nature, 453*, 650–653. doi:10.1038/nature06966

Lyons, K., Chabot, C.L., Mull, C.G., Holder, C.N.P. & Lowe, C.G. (2017). Who's my daddy? Considerations for the influence of sexual selection on multiple paternity in elasmobranch mating systems. *Ecology and Evolution, 7*, 5603–5612. doi:10.1002/ece3.3086

MacLure, M. (2013). Researching without representation? Language and materiality in post-qualititative methodology. *International Journal of Qualititative Studies in Education, 26*(6), 658–667.

Marcelo, P. (2015, May 21). Great white shark becomes Twitter star. *Smithsonian Teweentribune*. Retrieved from www.tweentribune.com/article/tween56/great-white-shark-becomes-twitter-star/

Masur, L.P. (1994). Reading Watson and the shark. *The New England Quarterly, 67*(3), 427–454.

McCoy, T. (2014, October 20). Scientists discover the awkward origins of sex. *The Washington Post*. Retrieved from www.washingtonpost.com/news/morning-mix/wp/2014/10/20/scientists-discover-the-kinda-disgusting-origins-of-sex/?utm_term=.ecc8b2c5d415

McHugh, S. (2012). Bitch, bitch, bitch: Personal criticism, feminist theory, and dogwriting. *Hypatia, 27*(3), 616–635.

McLean, I. (2016). *Rattling spears: A history of indigenous Australian art*. London: Reaktion Books.

Mearian, L. (2014, June 19). Katherine the white shark crashes research site's servers. *Computerworld*. Retrieved from www.computerworld.com/article/2491020/internet/katharine-the-white-shark-crashes-research-site-s-servers.html

Mearian, L. (2015, July 21). Some sharks have become social media stars. *Computerworld*. Retrieved from www.computerworld.com/article/2950514/social-media/some-sharks-have-become-social-media-stars.html

Megarry, J. (2014). Online incivility or sexual harassment? Conceptualising women's experiences in the digital age. *Women's Studies International Forum, 47*, 46–55.

Meijer, E. (2016). Speaking with animals: Philosophical interspecies investigations. In M. Tønnessen, K.A. Oma & S. Rattasepp (Eds.), *Thinking about animals in the age of the Anthropocene* (pp. 73–88). Lanham, MD: Lexington Books.

Mick Fanning shark attack memes (2015). [Video file]. Retrieved from www.youtube.com/watch?v=USwYN2gYKwI

Milman, O. (2015, July 20). 'Sharks don't like to eat people': Attack statistics contradict untested theories. *The Guardian*. Retrieved from www.theguardian.com/environment/2015/jul/20/sharks-dont-like-to-eat-people-attack-statistics-contradict-untested-theories

Morgan, M. (2017a, September 11). Terrified swimmers flee the water at Sydney's Manly beach after a GREAT WHITE SHARK washes up on shore—before do-gooders release the predator into a nearby ocean pool. *Daily Mail*. Retrieved from www.dailymail.co.uk/news/article-4871570/Shark-washes-Sydney-s-Manly-beach.html

Morgan, M. (2017b, September 12). *Great white shark called Fluffy who sent families fleeing in terror after washing up on Sydney's Manly beach to be released back into the wild after spending the night at an aquarium.* Retrieved from www.dailymail.co.uk/news/article-4874488/Shark-Fluffy-set-release-Sydney-s-Manly-Beach.html

Morgan, M. (2017c). *The heart-warming moment Sydney's favourite shark is released back into the wild after being rescued and spending the night in an aquarium.* Retrieved from www.dailymail.co.uk/news/article-4875996/Heart-warming-moment-Sydney-shark-released-wild.html

Morris, N. (2007). *The cinema of Steven Speilberg: Empire of light.* London: Wallflower Press.

Muter, B.A., Gore, M.L., Gledhill, K.S., Lamont, C. & Huveneer, C. (2012). Australian and U.S. news media portrayal of sharks and their conservation. *Conservation Biology, 27*(1), 187–196. http://dx.doi.org/10.1111/j.1523-1739.2012.01952.x

Nat Geo Wild (2013). *Shark seduction: World's deadliest* [Video file]. Retrieved from www.youtube.com/watch?v=34kpy3HB3RQ

Nature Video (2009, March 2). *The mother fish* [Video file]. Retrieved from www.youtube.com/watch?v=0r_2bH04YFc

Neale, M. (2000a). Lin Onus. *Artlink Magazine, 20*(1). Retrieved from www.artlink.com.au/articles/1394/lin-onus/

Neale, M. (2000b). Urban dingo. In M. Neale (Ed.), *Urban dingo: The art and life of Lin Onus 1948–1996* (pp. 11–23). Brisbane: Queensland Art Gallery.

Neff, C. (2012). Australian beach safety and the politics of shark attacks. *Coastal Management, 40*(1), 88–106.

Neff, C. & Hueter, R. (2013). Science, policy, and the public discourse of shark 'attack': A proposal for reclassifying human-shark interactions. *Journal of Environmental Studies and Sciences, 3,* 65–73.

Nielsen, J., Hedeholm, R.B., Jan Heinemeier, J., Bushnell, P.G., Christiansen, J.S., Olsen, J., . . . Steffensen, J.F. (2016). Eye lens radiocarbon reveals centuries of longevity in the Greenland shark (*Somniosus microcephalus*). *Science, 353*(6300), 702–704.

Noone, R. (2014, October 18). I screamed like hell. *The Daily Telegraph,* p. 4.

Noske, B. (1997). *Beyond boundaries: Humans and animals.* Montreal: Black Rose Books.

Orenstein, C. (2002). *Little Red Riding Hood uncloaked: Sex, morality, and the evolution of a fairytale.* New York: Basic Books.

Orenstein, C. (2004, Summer). Dances with wolves: Little Red Riding Hood's long walk in the woods. *Ms Magazine.* Retrieved from www.msmagazine.com/summer2004/danceswithwolves.asp

Orme, J. (2015). A wolf's queer invitation: David Kaplan's *Little Red Riding Hood* and queer possibility. *Marvels & Tales: Journal of Fairy-Tale Studies, 29*(1), 87–109.

Owen, D. (2009). *Shark: In peril in the sea.* Crows Nest, NSW: Allen & Unwin.

Page, F., Belot, H. & Westacott, B. (2014, April 4). Woman killed in shark attack two years after wharf warning. *Sydney Morning Herald,* p. 2.

Pardini, A.T., Jones, C.S., Noble, L.R., Kreiser, B., Malcolm, H., Bruce, B.D., . . . Marin, A.P. (2001, July 12). Sex-based dispersal of great white sharks. *Nature*, *412*, 139–140.

Peace, A. (2015). Shark attack! A cultural approach. *Anthropology Today*, *31*(5), 3–7.

Pennycook, A. (2018). *Posthumanist applied linguistics*. Abingdon, Oxon: Routledge.

Peschera, A. (2016). *Animal internet: Nature and the digital revolution*. Trans. E. Lauffer. New York: New Vessel Press.

Phillips, N. (2014, October 20). Ancient fish were first to have sex: But sideways. *The Sydney Morning Herald*. Retrieved from www.smh.com.au/technology/sci-tech/ancient-fish-were-first-to-have-sex--but-sideways-20141019-118b0y.html

Pierce, J. (2016). *Run, spot, run: The ethics of keeping pets*. Chicago: University of Chicago Press.

Plant, B. (2011). Welcoming dogs: Levinas and 'the animal' question. *Philosophy and Social Criticism*, *37*(1), 49–71.

Plumwood, V. (1993). *Feminism and the mastery of nature*. New York: Routledge.

Plumwood, V. (2012). *The eye of the crocodile*. Canberra: ANU E Press.

Potts, A. (2002). *The science/fiction of sex: Feminist deconstruction and the vocabularies of heterosex*. New York and London: Routledge.

Pratt, H.L. & Carrier, J.C. (2001). A review of elasmobranch reproductive behavior with a case study on the nurse shark, *Ginglymostoma cirratum*. *Environmental Biology of Fishes*, *60*, 157–188.

Pratt, M.L. (1992). *Imperial eyes*. New York: Routledge.

Pulver, D.V. (2016, March 29). Research group searches sea to tag, understand great white sharks. *Daytona Beach News Journal*. Retrieved from www.news-journalonline.com/article/LK/20160329/News/605067412/DN/

Queen's University Belfast (2007, May 23). No sex please, we're female sharks. *Science Daily*. Retrieved from www.sciencedaily.com/releases/2007/05/070523072254.htm

Quirke, A. (2002). *Jaws*. London: Palgrave Macmillan.

Ray, G. (2004). Little glass house of horrors. *Third Text*, *18*(2), 119–133.

Regan, T. (1983). *The case for animal rights*. Berkeley: University of California Press.

Robinson, N. & Nadin, M. (2014, April 4). Shark attack on swimmer jolts community out of its complacency. *The Australian*, p. 1.

Robson, F. (2015, November 28). Be alert, be afraid: The truth about shark attacks. *The Sydney Morning Herald*. Retrieved from www.smh.com.au/good-weekend/be-alert-be-afraid-the-truth-about-shark-attacks-20151124-gl78i6.html

Rose, D.B. & van Dooren, T. (2011). Guest editors' introduction. *Australian Humanities Review*, *50*, 1–4.

Ross, J. (2015, August 29). Protected killer sharks 'are lured towards humans'. *The Australian*, p. 3.

Rothwell, N. (2013, August 23). Special effects of the dance machine. *The Australian*. Retrieved from www.theaustralian.com.au/arts/special-effects-of-the-dance-machine/news-story/977ed6d9f9814920f80029340b333811

Roy, G. & Caudwell, J. (2014). Women and surfing spaces in Newquay, UK. In J. Hargreaves & E. Anderson (Eds.), *Handbook of sport, gender and sexuality* (pp. 235–244). Abingdon and New York: Routledge.

Roy Morgan Research (2015, April 23). *Surf's up! (For young women and 50+ folks, at least)*. Retrieved from www.roymorgan.com/findings/6202-surfs-up-for-young-women-fifty-plus-201504222329

Rubey, D. (1976). The *Jaws* in the mirror. *Jump Cut, 10/11*, 20–23. Retrieved from www.ejumpcut.org/archive/onlinessays/JC10-11folder/JawsRubey.html

Russell, K. (2017, January 18). Lonely female shark fights the patriarchy and gets pregnant without partner. *The Debrief*. Retrieved from www.thedebrief.co.uk/news/real-life/lonely-shark-gets-pregnant-without-partner-20170166283

Simpson, C. (2010). Australian eco-horror and Gaia's revenge: Animals, eco-nationalism and the 'new nature'. *Studies in Australasian Cinema, 4*(1), 43–54.

Snowden, K. (2010). Fairy tale film in the classroom. In P. Greenhill & S.E. Matrix (Eds.), *Fairy tale films* (pp. 157–177). Logan: Utah State University Press.

Solnit, R. (2014). *Men explain things to me*. Chicago: Haymarket Books.

Solnit, R. (2017). *The mother of all questions*. Chicago: Haymarket Books.

Stacey, D., Andrzejaczek, S. & Meekan, M. (2016, November 16). *Teenage male whale sharks don't want to leave home*. [Media release]. University of Western Australia. Retrieved from http://www.news.uwa.edu.au/201611169215/teenage-male-whale-sharks-dont-want-leave-home

Stedman, L. (1997). From Gidget to Gonad Man: Surfers, feminists and postmodernisation. *ANZJS, 33*(1), 75–90.

Stibbe, A. (2012). *Animals erased: Discourse, ecology and reconnection with the natural world*. Middletown, CT: Wesleyan University Press.

Stibbe, A. (2014). An ecolinguistic approach to critical discourse studies. *Critical Discourse Studies, 11*(1), 117–128.

Stibbe, A. (2015). *Ecolinguistics: Language, ecology and the stories we live by*. London: Routledge.

Streep, A. (2015). *The last hope of the great white shark?* Retrieved from www.outsideonline.com/1929746/last-hope-great-white-shark

Sturma, M. (1986). The great Australian bite: Early shark attacks and the Australian psyche. *The Great Circle, 8*(2), 78–81.

Sutherland, G., McCormack, A., Pirkis, J., Vaughan, C., Dunne-Breen, M., Easteal, P. & Holland, K. (2016). *Media representations of violence against women and their children: Final report* (ANROWS Horizons, 03/2016). Sydney: ANROWS.

Switek, B. (2014, October 19). Armored fish pioneered sex as you know it. *National Geographic*. Retrieved from https://news.nationalgeographic.com/news/2014/10/141019-fossil-fish-evolution-sex-fertilization/

Tench, W. (1793). *A complete account of the settlement at Port Jackson*. Retrieved from www.gutenberg.org/dirs/etext02/tsapj10.txt

Thompson, D. (2008). *The $12 million stuffed shark: The curious economics of contemporary art*. New York, NY: Palgrave Macmillan.

Tiffin, H. (2009). Sharks and the Australian imaginary. In S. Hosking, R. Hosking, R. Parnell & N. Bierbaum (Eds.), *Something rich and strange: Sea changes, beaches and the littoral in the Antipodes* (pp. 75–85). Kent Town, SA: Wakefield Press.

Tiffin, H. (2010). Shark. In M. Harper & R. White (Eds.), *Symbols of Australia: Uncovering the stories behind the myths* (pp. 67–73). Sydney: UNSW Press; Canberra: National Museum of Australia Press.

Toohey, K. (2018). The onto-epistemologies of new materialism: Implications for applied linguistics pedagogies and research. *Applied Linguistics*. doi:10.1093/applin/amy046

Torres, M.D. (2016). Havana's fortunes: 'Entangled histories' in Copley's *Watson and the shark*. *American Art, 30*(2), 8–13.

Torry, R. (1993). Therapeutic narrative: *The Wild Bunch, Jaws*, and Vietnam. *The Velvet Light Trap, 31*, 27–38.

Townsend, S. (2014, October 30). Ryan went to war against Jaws: Surfer tells of grapple with shark. *The Daily Telegraph*. Retrieved from www.dailytelegraph.com.au/

University of Illinois Chicago (2010). *Whale sharks may produce many litters from one mating, paternity test shows* [Media Release]. Retrieved from www.sciencedaily.com/releases/2010/08/100824184754.htm

van der Kooi, C.J. & Schwander, T. (2015). Parthenogenesis: Birth of a new lineage or reproductive accident? *Current Biology, 25*(15), R659–R661.

Vannini, P. (2014). Non-representational geography: New ways of animating lifeworlds. *Cultural Geographies, 22*(2), 317–327.

Vogel, C. (2006, October 1). Swimming with famous dead sharks. *The New York Times*. Retrieved from www.nytimes.com/2006/10/01/arts/design/01voge.html?page&_r=0

Waitt, G. (2008). 'Killing waves': Surfing, space and gender. *Social and Cultural Geography, 9*(1), 75–94.

Wajcman, G. (trans. P. Bradley) (2009). The animals that treat us badly. *Lacanian Ink, 33*, 126–145.

Walker, I. (2015, July 20). Fanning fights off killer shark in shock surf final. *Daily Telegraph*. Retrieved from www.dailytelegraph.com.au

West, J.G. (2011). Changing patterns of shark attacks in Australian waters. *Marine and Freshwater Research, 62*, 744–754.

Whatmough, S., Van Putten, I. & Chin, A. (2011). From hunters to nature observers: A record of 53 years of diver attitudes towards sharks and rays and marine protected areas. *Marine and Freshwater Research, 62*, 755–763.

White, L. (2013, Autumn). Damien Hirst's shark: Nature, capitalism and the sublime. *Tate Papers, 14*. Retrieved from www.tate.org.uk/research/publications/tate-papers/14/damien-hirst-shark-nature-capitalism-and-the-sublime

Winton, T. (2013). *Opinion: In deep water*. Retrieved from http://www/animals australia.org/media/opinion.php?op=374

Wolfe, N. (2018, September 24). *'Shameful': Four sharks culled after double Whitsundays attack*. Retrieved from www.news.com.au/

World Surf League (2015). *Shark attacks Mick Fanning at the J-Bay open 2015* [Video file]. Retrieved from www.youtube.com/watch?v=xrt27dZ7DOA&t=129s

Worm, B., Davis, B., Kettemer, L., Ward-Paige, C.A., Chapman, D., Heithaus, M.R., . . . Gruber, S.H. (2013). Global catches, exploitation rates, and rebuilding options for sharks. *Marine Policy, 40*, 194–204.

Yong, E. (2009, February 24). Male and female mako sharks separated by invisible line in the sea. *National Geographic* [Web Log Post]. Retrieved from http://phenomena.nationalgeographic.com/2009/02/24/male-and-female-mako-sharks-separated-by-invisible-line-in-the-sea/

Žižek, S. (Writer and Presenter) (2012). *The pervert's guide to ideology* [Motion Picture]. Blinder Films, UK.

Index

9 780367 728823